LOUISIANA STATE UNIVERSITY STUDIES

Humanities Series

Waldo McNeir, Editor

Leo B. Levy, Assistant Editor for this Number

————

Number Eight

Studies in American Literature

Second printing, 1962

LOUISIANA STATE UNIVERSITY STUDIES

Richard J. Russell, General Editor

The Louisiana State University Studies was established to publish the results of research by faculty members, staff, and graduate students of the University. Manuscripts of exceptional merit from sources other than aforementioned are considered for publication provided they deal with subjects of particular interest to Louisiana.

The Studies originally appeared as a unified series consisting of forty-two numbers, published between the years 1931 and 1941. In 1951 the Studies was reactivated, and is now being issued in the following series: Social Sciences, Humanities, Biological Sciences, Physical Sciences, and Coastal Studies. Other series may be established as the need arises.

The Studies in each series will be numbered only serially, without volume designation.

Requests for exchanges should be addressed to the Gift and Exchange Division, Louisiana State University Library, Baton Rouge. All other communications should be addressed to the Louisiana State University Press, Baton Rouge.

STUDIES IN
AMERICAN LITERATURE

Edited by

WALDO McNEIR

and

LEO B. LEVY

LOUISIANA STATE UNIVERSITY PRESS
BATON ROUGE

Contents

The Puritan Poet As Preacher–

An Edward Taylor Sermon

by
Donald E. Stanford

WHEN EDWARD TAYLOR died in 1729 in Westfield, Massachusetts, he was known as a very learned and distinguished preacher, although his preaching had usually been confined to his small village congregation. His friend of many years, the Puritan diarist Samuel Sewall, wrote: "I have heard him preach a Sermon at the Old South upon short warning which as the phrase in England is, might have been preached at Paul's Cross."[1] Today, his fame rests exclusively on his poetry, which had lain unread for many years in the Yale University Library until it was discovered by Thomas H. Johnson, who published selections from the lengthy manuscript in 1939.[2] Taylor's poems were first anthologized shortly before the publication of Johnson's edition by Norman Holmes Pearson and William Rose Benét;[3] his poetry has been included in almost every anthology of American verse since 1939, and he is now generally recognized as our most important colonial poet. Meanwhile, his sermons have been neglected, although there are fifteen of them extant in manuscript. They have never been published. Until recently, they have not even been read.[4]

Yet, a careful reading of these sermons is necessary to a full understanding of Taylor and his poetry; they are of considerable historical interest, and, if ever published, they will be a definite contribution to the sermonic literature of the period. Since Taylor's religious prose is virtually unknown, it will be worth while to analyze a representative sermon and to comment on the value of the sermons as contributory to a fuller understanding of the poetry.

1

Fourteen of these sermons, dated from October 26, 1701, to October 10, 1703, entitled *Christographia*[5] and bound by hand as a quarto volume, probably by Taylor himself, were presented to the Yale University Library by a descendant of the poet, Henry W. Taylor, in 1883. Another sermon, preached on the day of Taylor's ordination, August 27, 1679, is in the Westfield Church Record kept by Edward Taylor. The manuscript is owned by the Westfield Athenaeum.

The sermons of *Christographia* are carefully and logically constructed, all more or less on the same plan, and all are about the same length. Sermon 10 is typical of the others. It is about 11,400 words and covers in the manuscript 24 closely written pages. First, the Biblical text is announced—Eph. 1:23: "Which is his body, the fulness of him that filleth all in all." There follows an ecstatic comment on the truth of the text:

> O! what wonders is here. Hath God soe raised up Christs Humane body and so exalted the Humane Nature to be far above all Principalities, Might and Dominion and every name that is named both in this World and in the World to come and hath put all things under his feet? and hath made him head over all things unto the Church? and yet hath made the Church his Body and Fulness? What a strange thing is this? What unconceivable honour and advancement unto the Church is this? How can the Church be his Fulness who is so full of Advancement over all things in heaven and Earth? How Can the Church be said to fill him who indeed fills all things in all? But thus you see it is.

The Doctrine is then stated, "That there is in Christ an Ecclesiasticall fullness that the Church Constitutes in Christ." The Doctrine is briefly explained. There follow four Queries concerning this Doctrine, each Query being answered in minute detail. The Queries are:

1. "What Church is this thats Christs Fulness?"
2. "In what sense is the Church the Fulness of Christ?"
3. "What sort of Fulness is it of Christ that the Church is said to be?"
4. "What further Evidence may be presented to evince this, that the Church is Christs Fulness?"

The first Query is answered thus:

1. Negatively. "This Church doth not Consist of any painted, Flowerisht up or Hypocriticall Professours of Christianity. Such are rotten members of the visible body, but never had any union unto the Head of all."

2. Affirmatively. "This Church consists of the whole Body of the Elect of God both men and Angells, in all times and places of the world wheresoever."

The "Objection" is then raised: "How can the Holy Angells be members of this Church," and the answer is given in four "Solutions" which, summarized, state that angels, being in no need of redemption, do not have to be of the same nature as Christ to be members of the Church; Christ is head of angels as well as of men; Christ is redeemer only for elect people; yet angels are influenced by Christ's redemption.

Similarly, the second Query—"In what sense is the Church the Fulness of Christ?"—is answered in a series of "Solutions," an "Objection," and answers to the "Objection." A summary will be sufficient for our purposes. The Church is the fullness of Christ in an active and in a passive sense. In an active sense, Christ puts all his fullness into the Church as into a vessel; his electing Grace is poured into the Church alone—there is no Grace for those outside the Church; none of God's sunshine falls on any place but on his Church; Christ is mediator for the Church only and for none outside the Church; Christ's blood purchases salvation for the elect and the elect only. In a passive sense, Christ is a celestial vessel filled to the brim with the Church. Christ is the mystical head of the Church. The Church is the fullness of the body of Christ. The Church is also the inheritance of Christ, for an heir is the first-born son, and Christ was the first born of Mary.

The "Objection" is then raised: "But we finde him stiled Heir of all things (Heb. 1.2) . . . . Surely then his inheritance is extended larger than his Church." This is answered by three "Solutions." In summary: Christ inherits the heathen by way of conquest and rules them with a rod of iron; Christ's true inheritance is that which he cultivates (his Elect)—the rest he dashes to pieces; Christ has power over all, but he saves only his proper inheritance, the Church.

The third Query—"What sort of Fulness is it of Christ that the Church is said to be?"—is answered negatively and affirmatively. Negatively, it is not an internal fullness; affirmatively, it is his external fullness, as a man's riches are styled his external fullness.

The fourth Query—"What further Evidence may be presented to evince this, that the Church is Christs Fulness?"—is answered by two "Demonstrations": 1. "In that the Church is his own. He is the Lord Proprietor of it. He saith, My Vinyard which is mine is before mee. Can. 8. 12." There follow a number of quotations from Scripture to prove the point. 2. "In that the Church fills up severall Vacancies in Christ." Six ways are enumerated by which the Church fills up these "Vacancies." 1. God's Election—The entrance of sin seemed to evacuate the decree of Election, but the Church supplies this vacancy; 2. God's Wisdom—the Church fills the vacancy seemingly created in God's Wisdom by sin; 3. God's Glory—the vacancy created in the glory of God by sin is filled by the Church; 4. Redemption—the vacancy in the redemption made by Christ is supplied by the Church; 5. The promises of Christ—the promise that no good thing will be withheld from them that walk uprightly is made good by the Church; 6. Evangelical obedience and sanctifying grace—obedience to the law and the exercise of sanctified qualifications would not be possible without the Church of Christ.

The four Queries having been amply answered, the sermon concludes with four "Uses" of the Doctrine just defended and explicated.

Use 1. "By way of information." That the Church is the fullness of Christ will serve to discover the following truths: First, a glorious design of God touching some of the children of men, for God has designed to give some men an "Equality . . . if not a transcendencie above the Holy Angells," and further, God has designed that every one of his children shall make to the completing of Christ, for if Christ should have but one single child of God taken from him, he would not be full. God has designed that some men should be as necessary to Christ as Christ is to them. Secondly, every child of God will be honored as a fellow citizen with the saints. Thirdly, the perseverance of the saints is confirmed. The saints are members of Christ's body and Christ's body cannot lose its least member.

Use 2. "For Reproofe." First, this Doctrine means that the union between Christ and the Church is mystical and not physical; hence those Ubiquitarians (Lutherans and Papists) who believe in the carnal presence of Christ in the Lord's Supper are in error. Secondly, those that believe that while in a state of sin they can be members of Christ's Church are in error. Thirdly, this Doctrine brings a fearful charge against all such as are enemies and persecutors of the Church of Christ, for they shall be fearfully befooled; all attempts against God's children shall prove ineffectual; Christ will not see any of his children abused without avenging of it.

Use 3. "By way of Consolation to all the people of God." 1. They are in a safe state. They can no more fail of eternal joy than Christ can. 2. Christ has a high and wonderful love for them, for they are his body and no man ever hated his own body.

Use 4. "By Way of Exhortation." Let this Doctrine move us to a friendly carriage to all members of the Church of Christ. Those not of the mystical Body of the Church should strive to become members of this body. Those who by grace are members of Christ's fullness should be thankful to God and be ever pressing on to a fullness of obedience and holy walking with God.

Such are the substance and structure of a typical sermon by Edward Taylor. The doctrine is stated and affirmed; queries concerning the doctrine are raised and answered. The uses of the doctrine are set forth. Each point is emphasized by repetition and rephrasing so that the dullest in the congregation can understand it. There are, of course, frequent citations from Scripture—most of these are in English, although a few are in Hebrew, Greek, and Latin to impress the more learned members of the preacher's audience. In their solid logical structure Taylor's sermons are similar to many other Puritan sermons of the seventeenth and early eighteenth centuries. For example, Nathanael Mather's two sermons "The Righteousness of God through Faith" (London, 1694) are organized as follows: The text (Rom.3:22) is stated; the doctrine is derived from the text; the doctrine is cleared by answering three of six questions; the doctrine is applied under heading USE. In his second sermon, Mather follows a similar pattern, answering the three remaining questions of the six proposed in the first sermon and applying the doctrine with four "Uses." In a sermon by Henry

Flint, Fellow of Harvard, entitled "The Doctrine of the Last Judgment" (Boston, 1714), the text (Rom. 2:16) is stated; the doctrine derived from the text is cleared in four propositions and then applied in four "Uses." A similar pattern is followed in Urian Oakes's "The Soveraign Efficacy of Divine Providence" (Boston, 1682), which was delivered in Cambridge on September 10, 1677, on the occasion of an Artillery election.[6]

The structural model for these Puritan sermons may be found in William Perkins' "The Order and Summe of the sacred and onely Method of Preaching," which advises preachers:

1. To read the Text distinctly out of the Canonicall Scriptures.
2. To give the sense and understanding of it being read, by the Scripture it selfe.
3. To collect a few and profitable points of doctrine out of the naturall sense.
4. To apply (if he have the gift) the doctrines rightly collected, to the life and manners of men in a simple and plaine speech.[7]

Of a sermon by the English Puritan John Dod, W. Fraser Mitchell has written: "Preaching according to Dod's 'method,' it is evident, could not be expected to show literary grace. It was severely practical, directed to the great ends of convincing men of sin and instructing them in virtue."[8] And of New England sermons of the seventeenth century Samuel Eliot Morison says: "Their purpose was exegetical and practical. They exposed—'opened up' was their favorite phrase—a passage of Scripture; and on it expended their best art and skill. They drew on a wealth of theological learning for support and enforced their points by homely or startling phrases, and appeals to the imagination and emotions of the audience."[9] Both of these statements are true of Taylor's sermons. Their style is usually plain and straightforward, although there is a certain amount of theological jargon which is monotonous and sometimes incomprehensible to the modern reader. However, there are scattered passages of considerable eloquence which look forward to the magnificent rhetoric of Jonathan Edwards, although they never equal Edwards at his best. These are the passages that are of greatest interest to the modern reader and to students of Taylor's poetry, for they combine the sensuous and ingenious imagery of Taylor's poetic style with a sonorous prose cadence.

Taylor is at his most eloquent on two topics: the love of Christ for the elect and the terrors of the wrath of Christ toward the nonelect. Two passages on these topics follow. From Sermon 10:

> Christ hath high and Wonderfull Love for you. No man ever hated his own body but loved it. You are of Christs body and Fulness. You make to his Compleatness and glory. Surely then you are most deare to him and his love comes upon you; all the benefits that love can afford you come upon you. All the springs of Divine influences in the head shall be carried by the hand of Love down through all the secret wayes and Chanells of Convayances to every member of the body for its spirituall increase and fulness in that every member makes to the fulness of Christ so that Christs own fulness requires Christs keeping every member of his body full and his love Will mentain this and this is sweet Consolation. The Lord himselfe in Love to his Body hath died for it, that the beloved body might live and not dy and this love is extended to every member of the body. He sends down its Capitall Care over every member, spirituall for its spirituall nourishment, increase, growth and glory and these are managed so as conducts them safe through all Difficulties unto eternall glory.

The second passage is from Sermon 7:

> What a terrour will it be to thee to have Christ thine Enemy that is Almighty? O think of this. No terrour on this side hell like this. Can thy heart endure or thine hands be strong in the day that he shall deale with thee? Alass, if he come against thee in the form of a Lamb, though thou was the greatest Monarch or Mightiest mountain on earth, thou wouldst be ready to run into a mouse hole to hide thyselfe from his Wrath . . . He will put on Might as a garment and Majesty and strength as a Robe. He will array himselfe With glory and come in flames of fire to take Vengeance of his Enemies and revenge upon his Adversaries, to render his anger with fury and his rebukes with flames of fire. Now then what a terrour wilt thou be in when he shall thus come to deale with thee? Thinke of it. His Maje (s) ty shall be so great that the Angells of Glory Will shout at it, the Heavens Will ring again, the Aire and skies filld with his host will Quaver and the earth Will tremble, and now the most amazing sight that poor sinners set their Eyes on will appear before their

eyes to their utter Confusion. Thou mayst as easily toss away the earth as a tennis ball or turn the World out of doores as a puppy dog or Pull down the Heavens over the heads of all things as a tilt Cloath, as easily recover the time that is passt away, Weigh the Whole Empyreall battlements in a pair of Gold Scales, Contain the Winde in the Hollow of thy hande and lade the Sea dry with an acorn bowle as stand before the Lord Jesus Christ who is Almighty and thine Enemy.

A careful reading of all of Taylor's sermons should settle various arguments which have arisen concerning the orthodoxy of his poetry. It is my own conviction, after examining all of Taylor's extant manuscripts and after reading all of Taylor's extant poetry and sermons, that his theology was in complete agreement with the accepted doctrine of New England as formulated in the Westminster Confession,[10] and that this doctrine can properly be described as Calvinism because it is identical with Calvin's *Institutes* in all important matters.[11] This view differs from prevailing scholarly opinion. Samuel Eliot Morison states that none of the seventeenth-century Puritans were Calvinists: " . . . after reading some hundreds of puritan sermons, English and New English, I am about ready to deny that the New England puritans were predestinarian Calvinists."[12] Professor Morison repeats this assertion in his revised edition of the Pronaos.[13] Perry Miller has also stated that Jonathan Edwards was the first New England Calvinist,[14] and Thomas H. Johnson writes in a similar vein: "Calvinism was never synonymous with puritanism. Archbishop Whitgift, who crowned James I, was a Calvinist; but not so the men he drove to seek out a new plantation in the Bay Colony."[15]

Furthermore, quite aside from the question as to whether or not the New England theology can properly be called Calvinism, several scholars have maintained that Taylor was not in accord with the theology of his contemporaries. Kenneth Murdock has said that Taylor lacked a sense of personal sin[16] and that his attitude toward the Lord's Supper was unorthdox with respect to the doctrine of the real presence.[17] Herbert Blau considers Taylor unorthodox with respect to the Lord's Supper[18] and so does S. E. Lind.[19] Perry Miller appears to be somewhat inconsistent on the subject of Taylor's orthodoxy. In *The New England Mind: From Colony to*

Province he writes: "He [Taylor] took no part in politics, and was not, as was Bulkeley, a rebel against the Congregational order; but in some deeper sense, he too was out of touch—and consciously —with the system that emerged from the Revolution. He too turned inward, pouring out his anxiety in a verse technique that Puritans considered suitable only to the sensualities of the Church of England. . . . he alone raised his eyes to the universe, and asked the stupendous question of who, in this cosmic bowling alley, bowled the sun?"[20] With respect to the stupendous question Taylor asked concerning the cosmic bowling alley, it should be mentioned that the question is merely rhetorical and is answered by Taylor himself a few lines later in his Preface to *Gods Determinations*. The answer, of course, is God. In his most recent statement on Taylor, Professor Miller seems to have no doubts of Taylor's orthodoxy. He writes: "From his poetry we see that he was a thoroughly orthodox federalist theologian."[21]

Of particular importance to our understanding of Taylor's theology is his concept of the Elect, a concept which is made quite clear in Sermon 10. Thomas H. Johnson suggests a universalistic tendency in Taylor's thinking when, in his glossary of his edition of Taylor's poems, he states: "His [God's] sole desire was that man should achieve the happiness which was the end for which he was created, and which he alone of all creatures was capable of achieving, since mankind possessed such stock of inherent grace as, by improvement, was capable of winning felicity. . . . By the terms of the Covenant of Grace, God assured salvation to all who fulfilled the imposed condition of faith. Hence the emphasis, among covenant professors, was felt to be rather upon the ability of all to be saved than upon God's predetermined election of a select few."[22] Further, defining "inherent grace" Johnson writes: "That implantation of grace with which all men are born, and which by improvement is capable of winning men salvation."[23] There are, I believe, two misconceptions here. Taylor believed that only the Elect possessed inherent grace, not all mankind. Furthermore, Taylor did not emphasize in his sermons the ability of all to be saved. Only members of the Church were to be saved, a doctrine expressed, as has been shown, in Sermon 10.

Miss Willie T. Weathers carries Johnson's suggestion to its ex-

treme conclusion when she argues, in her analysis of Taylor's poem
Gods Determinations, that Taylor was a universalist—that he believed that all mankind would be saved. She writes: "Although the
title is *Gods Determinations Touching His Elect*, the poem deals
with the salvation of *all* mankind . . . the term 'Elect' becomes
synonymous with the 'All mankinde' who were split into the original dichotomy."[24] A reading of Sermon 10 (and a more careful
reading of *Gods Determinations*) would have prevented these misconceptions. Taylor makes his position quite clear that Christ
saves the Elect and the Elect only. And he makes quite clear that
the Elect are only a part of mankind:

> All the Whole Bundle of the Shining Beams of Executive
> Love in the Godhead, streame forth through Christ upon the
> Church onely. This sun shines onely upon that plot. This
> Goshan hath all the light of that sun, not one beame runs be-
> yond these bounds. None of this sunshine falls upon any other
> field. The Church is the Onely Object of the boundless Love
> of Gods infinite breast. God so Loved the World i.e. the Elect
> World and not the world opposed to the Elect.
> All the Works of Redemption that Christ hath Carried on are
> all bestowed upon the Church. There is not one of them be-
> stowed any other way. Christ put not forth one mediatoriall
> act, one Work of Mediation, one design of Redemption, one
> Drop of his precious blood, One breath of his interceding Func-
> tion, or one minim of his headship influences for any that is not
> of his Body the Church as he included his petitions within the
> Walls of his Church. So he excluded all out of his Church out
> of his Petitions. Joh. 17.9. And as he would not pray for the
> World, so he would not poure out his Soule unto death for the
> World. But all is for his Church.

In his sermons as in his poetry, Taylor was operating within the
bounds of a narrow, dogmatic Calvinism. And, indeed, it was
his rigid Calvinism which motivated his most powerful writing in
poetry and prose. For he was convinced he was of the Elect, and
for the Elect, double predestination has no terror, but rather an
overwhelming conviction of the mercy, the sweetness, and the
glory of God.

Nationalism and Aesthetics in the *North American Review:* 1815-1850

by
Darwin Shrell

FOR THE AMERICAN critic living in the formative years of this republic, nationalism and aesthetics posed a hard dilemma. National pride in many instances led the critic to call for a literature based upon unique American materials and experiences, but the critic's training forced him to judge American works in the light of traditions and critical principles which were largely English and European in origin. The resultant conflict constitutes an important chapter in American literary history, as Benjamin T. Spencer's recent book proves.[1] The intensity of that conflict and the complexity of the search for a solution are brought into sharp focus within the issues of a single literary journal. Thus it is possible to observe within the limits of the *North American Review*, 1815-1850, some record of the critical efforts to balance nationalism and aesthetics and to identify the materials and symbols from which a national literature might be created.

In at least two respects the *North American Review* is an important source of information about early nineteenth-century American critics. From 1815, the date of its first issue, until the mid-nineteenth century the *Review* was—in spite of its Cambridge and Boston orientation—the national literary journal most widely read and discussed by American intellectuals. Its list of contributors included most of the leading writers and critics of the period. Furthermore, from its first issues the *Review* voiced its concern over the state of the nation's literature. "Our literary delinquency

may principally be resolved into our dependence on English literature," William Tudor, first editor of the journal, wrote. "We have
been so perfectly satisfied with it that we have not made an attempt towards a literature of our own."[2]

Under the initial direction of William Tudor, 1815-1817, and
during the subsequent editorships, 1818-1855, of Jared Sparks, Edward Channing, Edward Everett, Alexander H. Everett, Francis
Bowen, and Andrew J. Peabody, the *Review* continued to express
nationalistic sentiments. In 1820 the *Edinburgh Review* (XXXIV,
67, 161) called its readers' attention to the *North American Review*, which it identified as the most promising production from an
American press. "Though abundantly patriotic, or rather national, there is nothing offensively or absolutely unreasonable in the
tone of its politics. . . ," the Scottish magazine concluded. Nationalism and sound scholarship were, as the *Edinburgh Review* had
recognized, the distinctive characteristics of the *North American
Review*.

There were, among the contributors to the *Review*, two distinct
nationalistic attitudes. The first, shared by most of the contributors,
was the conviction that through sound scholarship and judgment
the magazine could bring recognition for the American critic
while acquainting the reader with the most important books of
America, England, and Europe. The second attitude, expressed by
the most persistent exponents of literary nationalism, sought to
justify the use of natural American scenes in literature and art.
Upon this second attitude, which is the subject of special interest in this study, the contributors to the *Review* were sharply
divided, for during the first thirty years of its existence the journal found itself torn between two contradictory standards of critical principles.

The first, in order of time, were the critical ideas which had
dominated a great portion of eighteenth-century English literature. Joseph Story, Edward Everett, Alexander Hill Everett, William Ellery Channing, George Ticknor, and many other early
contributors to the *Review* had passed the formative period of
their adult reading under the influence of Dryden, Pope, Addison,
Steele, and Swift. From these and other English neoclassicists many
contributors to the *Review* drew their conclusions about the na-

ture and purpose of literature. Concerned with universals, they expressed little interest in literature based upon regional characteristics. Seeking to idealize the familiar, they shunned striking individuals, wild forests, and unusual landscapes. Their models, when they sought to copy nature, were taken from ancient Greece.

The import of this attitude was a disregard for the new. A young nation, situated amid the grandeurs of uncultivated nature and settled by uneducated people, offered little of interest to the neoclassic critic in the *Review*. It was precisely the values most dear to a great body of Americans—individualism, belief in progress, appreciation for grandeur, love of wildness, and a disregard for ancient history—for which the neoclassic critics in the *Review* found least philosophic and artistic justification. Such neoclassic attitudes were prominent in the *Review*. They appeared in the articles of Franklin Dexter, Samuel Gilman, Livi Frisbie, Francis William Winthrop, John Chipman Gray, William Loring, John Pickering, Edward Everett, A. M. Fisher, George Bancroft, Alexander H. Everett, Andrews Norton, and Francis W. P. Greenwood. Although this list does not include all the neoclassic contributors, it does represent some of the most eloquent and forceful exponents of that school.

The pronouncements of this group echo the literary convictions of the eighteenth century. In a review, "Airs of Palestine; A Poem by John Pierpont, Esq" (March, 1817), Franklin Dexter found little worth in the "ballad-mongers and song-wrights [*sic*]" in modern poetry and lamented the passing of the heroic couplet (VI, 411). Pre-occupation with established literary form led Edward Everett to hope in 1821 that the best genius of the age would not go into novel writing (XIII, 393). Two years earlier William Loring had directed a pointed rebuke at America's literary nationalists (IX, 26-35). Of those critics demanding more American interest in ancient Greek art and literature, Edward Everett, editor of the *Review* from 1820 to 1823, was the most active. In the January, 1821, issue of the magazine, Everett placed the blame for America's literary immaturity upon a neglect of classical art. "It need not be said," he contended, "that the insensibility to this species of beauty and the want of the deeper and finer insight into the whole ancient character, which results from this insensibility, are great defects in our education in this country; defects that call aloud for remedy" (XII, 187).

In the *Review* England's romantic poets received a cool reception from neoclassic critics. Discussing Southey and Wordsworth in the January, 1823, issue of the magazine, Samuel Gilman noted "a disinclination in these authors to consult the precise intellectual tone and spirit of the average mass to whom their works are presented" and ascribed to them an inability or inaptitude "to infuse into their writings a tone precisely harmonizing with the natural inclinations and principles of taste implanted in the general mind" (XVI, 103). In 1825 both Alexander H. Everett and Andrews Norton attacked Byron's poetry on the ground that it outraged the universal tastes of men; both saw elements of decay in modern poetry (XX, 1-47; XXI, 300-359). One militant neoclassicist, William B. O. Peabody, continued as late as 1830 to maintain that Pope had carried the sweetness and harmony of English verse to a degree of excellence unknown before or since (XXXI, 109).

More than fifty major articles during the first period of the *Review*, 1815-1830, reveal strong currents of neoclassic thought which signify an aesthetic rejection of the American scene. Evidences of this rejection are abundant. Walter Channing, in an essay, "On the Fine Arts," July, 1816, found the American scene an unfit subject for great art.

> Have we in fact [he asked] enough that is peculiar in this country? Our country has, it is true, every variety of surface, and the vegetable productions of all climates. Its mountains are lofty, and its woods majestick—its lakes are lost in distance, before the eye which would paint them. But would not the landscape painter, who would leave the regions of cultivation, to give his pencil to the simple service of nature, be in danger of returning to us with his canvass loaded with a thousand woods, or washed by an interminable sea? Would there not be some hazard, that amid such luxuriance in nature, such magnificent confusion, an indistinctness of mental vision would be produced, or that the best exertions that genius might make, would be sacrificed to an affected fidelity? (III, 198).

Channing maintained that America's many strange and wonderful sights were no incentive to the artist. He believed that art's higher purpose was to teach through the medium of universally known ideas and customs, rather than to amuse by portraying the strange features of our land or "unknown habits of our peasants." "How many of these sources of interest must be wanting," he lamented, "to the native artist, who confines himself to our country. His pictures will want novelty—They will not extend our knowledge" (III, 199).

The dismissal of the common and the uncultivated in nature extended to the common people: frontiersmen, settlers, and rural folk. In a review, "The Red Rover," December, 1818, Grenville Mellen gave this evaluation of the importance of the settler as a subject for American literature:

> Moreover the elements of society, considered *implicitly* as the society among the early settlements of this country, offer little in the shape of sects or classes, that is calculated to meet and satisfy the popular taste. . . . but it will be said, if we have anything like legendary lore, we must seek for it among the children of the forest, for the good reason that it is nowhere else to be found. But there is a fallacy in this. We belong as a people to the English school of civilization. It is not necessary that the scene of an American work of imagination should be laid in America. . . . It is a mistaken idea, also, that to constitute an American novel, either the scene must be laid in the early wilderness of this country, or that events of so recent date as those connected with our revolution, must occupy a prominent portion of its pages (VIII, 135).

One by one the neoclassicists dismissed as unworthy subjects for art and literature the most characteristic aspects of the American scene: the Revolutionary War, the environment of the frontier, the Indians, and the settlers. To these men a formidable barrier separated the American scene from art. Although they praised nationalism in economics and politics, they could find no place for it in literature.

The neoclassic critic's rejection of the American scene in literature did not go unchallenged, however. Even in its early issues the *Review* contained essays which showed a movement in the opposite direction. Most, if not all, of the ideas constituting this movement were taken from English, French, and German romanticists. Such *Review* contributors as William Cullen Bryant, William Tudor, John Knapp, and Howard Gardiner—to name a few—found in the romantic movement a critical yardstick favorable to the uncultivated American scene. In applying this measure, they took from English and European romanticists a stronger reliance on the importance of the emotions, more emphasis upon subjective reactions to nature, and less belief in the universal reason of man. They borrowed, also, the whole body of loosely related ideas or romanticisms which appeared most prominently in the literature of the romanticists.[3] The pages of the *Review* from 1815 through 1850 reveal sixteen of the most persistent romanticisms, ideas expressing appreciation for the (1) strange and exotic, (2) irregular and ornate, (3) wild and rough, (4) unsophisticated, (5) naive and intuitive, (6) sentimental, (7) melancholy, (8) solitary, (9) spontaneous, (10) humanitarian, (11) remote in time, (12) varied and diverse, (13) democratic, (14) independent, (15) prolific or fruitful, (16) sublime.

It is not practicable to list all of the articles or poems that expressed these attitudes in the *Review*, for such selections are numerous. William Cullen Bryant's "Thanatopsis," published for the first time in the September, 1817, issue of the *Review* and his "To a Waterfowl," which appeared in the same magazine three decades later, emphasized melancholy and intuitive knowledge. Literary critics were enthusiastic over Sir Walter Scott's medieval revival; they praised the Gothic elements which not only were important in Scott's novels but were a stock in trade for numerous lesser writers.[4] Supporters of Lord Byron made numerous professions of admiration, in the *Review*, for the poet's use of the strange and exotic, the unusual, the spontaneous, the varied, and the solitary.[5] Up to 1845, twenty-three major reviews of Byron's life or works appeared in the *North American Review*. It is significant, however, that only six articles on Byron appeared before 1821, and at least half of these were not favorable. Between 1821 and 1845 seventeen articles were devoted to Byron, and these reflected a larger proportion of favorable opinion. By 1830, Byron's romanticisms were regarded as aesthetically acceptable.

In a similar manner the critics for the *Review* singled out for praise Cooper's use of the vastness of the American forests, his appreciation for the wild and rough in external nature, his creation of unsophisticated and primitive characters, and his pictures of fruitful American forests, filled with a plenitude of game and food.[6] With equal enthusiasm Francis W. P. Greenwood, William H. Prescott, and William Phillips approved the democratic and humanitarian ideas of Wordsworth and William Godwin. Though such critics were in the minority until 1830, these samplings from critical opinion indicate romantic inclinations in the *Review*.

The romanticists' fondness for the wild, rough, and vast in nature emphasized characteristics which abounded in the American scene; yet these characteristics existed, to some extent, in all countries. For the literary nationalist there remained still the question of aesthetic justification for a purely national literature.

A system of justification was available to the Boston critics, however. In 1815 a revised edition of Archibald Alison's *Essays on the Nature and Principles of Taste* (1790) was published in Boston by Cummings and Hillard, the firm which took over publication of the *North American Review* in 1817. Alison, an advocate of association psychology, approached the aesthetic principles of taste and beauty in terms of man's previous experience. He contended that all knowledge, from the simplest to the most complex ideas, came from associations built around physical sensations. In brief, man's intellectual and emotional character is the result of his environment and experience, the physical sensations he derives from them, and the association of ideas he builds around these sensations. The importance of environment in man's appreciation of beauty led Alison to an open endorsement of nationalism.

Robert Streeter's study of Archibald Alison's influence upon the *North American Review* traces reflections of Alison's association psychology in a large number of *Review* articles.[7] As Streeter demonstrates, the appeal of Alison's theories rested upon his assumptions about the nature of beauty. "For the associationists," Streeter observes, "beauty was not an abstract quality transcending national boundaries. For them, a literary work became beautiful when it appealed to the associations which varied from nation to nation, even as they did from person to person."[8] Alison's assumptions did more than offer critical respectability to nationalism; they suggested purposes for some of the basic premises of the romantic movement.

In the *Review* some of the most vocal exponents of association psychology and literary nationalism were William Tudor, John Knapp, William Cullen Bryant, Julian Crommerlin Verplanck, Samuel Gilman, William H. Gardiner, and Walter Channing. The pronouncements of Knapp and Bryant illustrate how this group sought to provide aesthetic justification for literature which took its material from national environment. John Knapp's "National Poetry," published in the December, 1818, issue of the *Review*, is a good example. In this essay Knapp called attention to the rich backgrounds of American scenery and history which had produced a strong association of national ideas. These were the ingredients for a national literature, he maintained, adding this opinion: "If men's minds are influenced by scenes in which they are conversant, Americans can scarcely be denied a claim to be inspired with some peculiar moral graces, by their grand and lovely landscapes. But moreover, it is beneficial to connect our best intellectual associations with places in our own land. In part, we love our country because our minds seem to have been furnished with its surface, and because our most natural and vivid ideas are inseparable from pictures which have it for their groundwork" (VIII, 174). In much the same spirit Bryant attacked those neoclassic critics who disparaged American scenes in literature. "The peculiarities in the manners and the character of our countrymen, have too long been connected with ideas merely low and ludicrous ..., " he wrote. "It is time, however, that they were redeemed from these gross and degrading associations."[9]

Whether the contributors to the *Review* took their literary theories of association from Alison or other sources, they had found the critical dialectic by which they could defend a purely national literature. A question remained, however; what materials and symbols could best represent the American scene?

The quest for symbols and materials brought a variety of responses. In the September, 1815, issue of the *Review*, Walter Channing called attention to the "oral literature of the aborigines" as the most original literature in America.[10] Edward T. Channing's essay, "On Models in Literature" (July, 1816), called for "native-ness, despite its rudeness" (III, 207). Richard H. Dana, Sr., a thorough romantic, praised the commonplace.[11] William Tudor's essay, "Miss Huntley's Poems" (May, 1815), was more specific in identifying subjects for a national literature. "We have in the way of subjects, a rich and various mine that has hardly been opened. Let it be remembered, how much the genius of Scott has struck out from his Scottish highland chiefs, and the border warfare with England . . . . How much more important, how much more varied, how vastly superior in picturesque effect, the events that took place on our frontiers, in the course of the seventeenth and the beginning of the eighteenth century" (I, 120). In addition to the frontier, Tudor listed as good subject for a national literature the American Indians, the great variety of classes in America—ranging from those colonists who belonged to French or English nobility to the most humble settler—early American battles, and: " . . . then the magnificence of the scenery,—the cataract, in its gigantick magnificence, that might receive all the waterfalls of Europe united, without perceiving the addition; the lakes whose shores for a century and a half, have been rendered illustrious by so many memorable combats of different nations . . . " (I, 120). Later that year in an "Address Delivered to the Phi Beta Kappa Society of Cambridge," Tudor repeated this catalogue of subjects suitable for a national literature and added a new topic, native animals, to the list (II, 18).

In the December, 1818, issue of the magazine John Knapp's "National Poetry" stressed the Revolution, the frontier, and external nature as materials for a national literature (VIII, 169-176). John G. Palfrey in a review of "Yamayden" (April, 1821), suggested as the material for a national literature the experiences of the stern Puritans "coming in conflict with the relentless wilderness" (XII, 480). William H. Gardiner listed, in his review of Cooper's *The Spy*, July, 1822, the presettlement period in America, the Indian wars, and the Revolution (XV, 281); and in the April, 1825, issue of the *Review*, William Cullen Bryant praised the spirit of democratic equalitarianism which enabled America to develop a variety of characters capable of giving life to a strong national literature (XX, 272).

A survey of the articles advocating literary nationalism reveals that the frontier and the American Indian were the most frequently mentioned subjects. The associationists justified their selection of the frontier upon the grounds that it had been a region of conflict; therefore, many of the nation's strong associations of national pride revolved around it. The persistence of the "frontier" or "wilderness" themes in American literature from Cooper's *The Pioneers* to Faulkner's "The Bear" verifies the predictions of the early literary nationalists.

The factors which made the frontier and wilderness appealing —individualism, variety, the remote in time, wildness in nature, and cultural primitivism—were unacceptable to the neoclassicists. The subjects of the American frontier, as much as any other topic in the *Review*, drew a sharp line of demarcation between neoclassic and romantic critics. The division of opinion upon this subject reflects, rather accurately, the strength and period of each group among the editors and contributors. William Tudor, the first editor, was torn between both schools of literary principles. Editors Jared Sparks and Edward Channing were favorable to the general romantic movement, and Edward Everett, another editor, was neoclassic in taste. In the magazine between 1815 and 1835, the fifty major articles expressing neoclassic preferences are matched by an equal number written by romantic critics. Statistically there appears to be a balance of critical opinion in the magazine during its first twenty years. Harry Hayden Clark arrived at such a conclusion after a study of 231 critical reviews in the *North American Review* from 1815 to 1835.[12] However, if one examines the dates of the articles Clark reviewed, one discovers that most of those written by romantic critics appeared around 1830. The prominence of neoclassic opinions in the *Review* up to 1825 overshadowed the literary nationalism of the romanticists.

In spite of the sustained strength of the neoclassicists during the first twenty years of the *Review*, a pattern of literary nationalism appeared in the growing number of romantic reviews. Knapp, Tudor, Bryant, Channing, and their associates found in associationism the justification for a national literature, and in a systematic manner they called the attention of their readers to the native features about which this literature could be written. These features related to what the romantic critics in the *Review* regarded as the unique feature of American experience, the frontier.

On the subjects of nationalism and aesthetics, the *Review* reflects two significant developments: the late triumph of romanticism in the magazine and the type of literary and artistic nationalism advocated in the *Review*. Up to 1830 the cautious—often suspicious— attitude of the *Review* toward the romantic literature of the period placed the magazine in opposition to some of the leading romanticists of the period and encouraged its readers to share this attitude. Although one cannot prove that the *Review* slowed the rise of romanticism in American literature, the facts are abundant that it did not give it sustained critical help or support before 1825. More important, however, was the type of nationalism seen in the *Review*. Almost without exception the literary nationalists were concerned with American things (the frontier, the wilderness, the Indians) rather than ideas. Aside from the theory of associationism, which did little more than justify American settings, there was no new and basic philosophy about which the writer could weave his materials.

The accomplishments of the *Review* should not be minimized, however. Slowly and persistently the literary nationalists had focused the attention of their readers upon the need for a national literature and upon the artistic merits of the American scene. When the west finally spoke, in the voices of Twain, Harte, and Garland, there is little doubt that the *Review* was shocked by what they said; yet a record of almost half a century of literary nationalism linked the *Review* with the western school.

Emerson's Political Quandary

by
Otis B. Wheeler

IT IS FAIRLY easy to establish what Ralph Waldo Emerson said and did about political and economic questions of his time; it is not so easy to explain some of the statements and actions of this "wisest American" according to any consistent political or philosophical system. Certainly the essay "Politics," when read with an awareness of the facts of Emerson's life and the intimate details of his journals, falls short of the full, consistent statement one would like. Nor is there much help from the aphorism, often true of simpler men, that a conservative is a radical grown old. As will be seen, his views shift from time to time, but not according to any consistent pattern of chronology. In fact, on some issues his attitudes might be better described as continuously ambivalent rather than shifting.

Perhaps the best testimony to the difficulty of fitting Emerson into any mold is the variety of attempts that have been made to do just that, with supporting evidence drawn from the Emerson canon. He has been called a "radical," an "anarchist," a "nihilist," a "radical democrat," and "the philosopher of democracy."[1] A less doctrinaire approach sees him as superior to politics, disillusioned with both the Whigs and the Democrats, and not too confident of the Republicans.[2] Still another view attempts to reconcile the apparent contradiction of his commitment in his actions to the competitive economy and the conservative money system of the Whigs, and his commitment in his writings to the brotherhood of man and the Oneness of the Universe. The apparent contradiction is seen as a consistent expression of the dual law of which he speaks in

"Ode to Channing"—law for thing and law for man. On a material level it is right that the law for thing should hold; on a spiritual level the law for man must rule.[3]

If these variant attempts to put him into a consistent pattern represent degrees of error, as I believe, the error stems largely from the tendency to regard Emerson too exclusively as a philosopher. For we justly expect from a philosopher a certain intellectual rigor. But we are coming more and more to admit that Emerson is primarily a poet and that even in his prose it is the poetic quality rather than the philosophic rigor that most readers admire. Poetry and poets are necessarily emotional; and Emerson, outwardly calm and undemonstrative—even a bit bloodless to an observer like Hawthorne—is at bottom a highly emotional man, a man of strong family attachments and humanitarian sympathies. Why should we be reluctant to admit that he was sometimes emotional about politics and economics too? Such an admission, it may be argued, detracts from his Olympian stature. Perhaps so. To admit that his political and economic opinions are sometimes related unconsciously to his social status, his family background, his personal interests, and his humanitarian feelings does make him more human. It also makes him more understandable, particularly when these factors are seen interacting with certain of his fundamental doctrines such as individualism and compensation.

The best way to see this is to examine some of his comments, first, about issues and, second, about political leaders of his period.

I

Emerson's quandary is epitomized in his often-quoted judgment that the Democrats had the best cause and the Whigs had the best men.[4] If, as he says repeatedly in other contexts, parties and states are just individuals writ large, one would expect the best men to have the best policies. But not so. Take, for instance, the tariff policy of the Whigs as opposed to the free-trade position of the Democrats. On this issue, Emerson held with the latter, partly because it was consonant with his doctrine of compensation. In the essay of that name (1841) he wrote almost a paraphrase of Adam

Smith's famous "invisible hand" passage. "Our action is overmastered and characterized above our will by the laws of nature. We aim at a petty end quite aside from the public good, but our act arranges itself by irresistible magnetism in a line with the poles of the world."[5] It is not surprising, then, to hear him speak out in "Politics" (1844) for free trade as a party doctrine: "The philosopher, the poet, the religious man, will of course wish to cast his vote with the democrat [sic] for free trade . . . . "[6] But his subsequent references to free trade were less positive. In his journal for 1851 he wrote, "Free Trade must be right . . . . But I think we shall never understand political economy until we get Béranger or Burns or some great poet to teach it in songs."[7] (Note here the reliance on poetry above philosophy!) In his 1868 journal he candidly admitted that he knew nothing about trade, and that "there is not the sciolist who cannot shut my mouth and my understanding by strings of facts that seem to prove the wisdom of tariffs. But my faith in freedom of trade, as the rule, returns always."[8] All this reveals that though he stood with the Democrats for free trade, he was never sure of the economic grounds of his belief. Whatever intellectual grounds he might have had would come from the implied justification of *laissez faire* in his doctrine of compensation.

The recurring question of the United States Bank, Emerson seems to have ignored. But his views on the related question of hard money and speculative finance again placed him generally in sympathy with the Democrats. Though inflation and deflation were always a puzzle to him, he saw clearly that "Bank-notes rob the public."[9] On speculation his views had a more personal reference, resulting from his own loss of some money in railroad stock. In his journal for 1857 he wrote with wry humor, "I took such pains not to keep my money in the house, but to put it out of reach of burglars by buying stock, and had no guess that I was putting it into the hands of these very burglars now grown wiser and standing dressed as Railway directors."[10] Of course this objection to speculation on the grounds of danger to the investor, in this case himself, took no account of the broader Democratic objection on the grounds of damage to the national economy.

The humanitarian impulse was probably behind Emerson's

support of the Democratic movement for penal-code reform, of which the most important aspect was the abolition of imprisonment for debt. Reduction of the number of crimes to which capital punishment might apply and various improvements in the prison regimen were also pushed through—nearly all of these things during the thirties. At the end of that decade Emerson found these reforms good, for he was still speaking out "with the democrat . . . for the abolition of legal cruelties in the penal code."[11]

In the matter of Abolition the development of Emerson's feelings is too well known to warrant detailing the process again. It will suffice to say that his early aloofness toward the movement gradually changed to warm support. Though never condoning slavery, Emerson required the emotional impact of such events as the Compromise of 1850, passage of the Fugitive Slave Law and the Kansas-Nebraska Bill, and the martyrdom of John Brown to bring him out as an ardent supporter of Abolition. That he distrusted his own motives is to be seen in his occasional tendency to draw back from the movement, almost to wonder how he became involved. In 1852 he wrote in his journal, "In hours of sanity I recover myself . . . . I have quite other slaves to free than those negroes, to wit, imprisoned spirits, imprisoned thoughts . . . which, important to the republic of Man, have no watchman, or lover, or defender, but I."[12] This emotion that he distrusted is the dominant quality of his impassioned denunciation of the Fugitive Slave Law: "It is a filthy enactment. I shall not obey it, by God."[13] The sublime example of individualism in John Brown's martyrdom brought forth eulogies that ring with emotion. No more than most other men of the time could Emerson deny the warm humanitarian impulses in his breast, even if it meant forsaking temporarily the high resolve to free men's minds first.

Perhaps the most fundamental political issue in Emerson's lifetime was the extension of suffrage, with the Whigs on the side of limitation and the Democrats on the side of extension. For our purposes, the question boils down to this: Did Emerson have faith in the virtue and wisdom of the common people? The answer is that he did and he did not; it is a very revealing confusion.

It is easy to forget that in pre-Civil-War America class barriers were much more influential in the life and thinking of even the liberal-minded individual than they are today, and that the frontier rather than the settled areas was the main source of the egalitarian spirit of Jacksonian Democracy. Emerson, with his Brahmin background, naturally and instinctively placed a premium on good breeding, education, and cultivated intelligence—qualities which were anything but prevalent among the lower classes. For the same reason he was relatively insensitive to the redeeming camaraderie that Whitman could see in them. In his spontaneous reactions to *hoi polloi*, then, he often reflected the estrangement that was the result of his being the Reverend William Emerson's son.

Good manners, for instance, always meant a great deal to him. As a very young man he unfavorably compared the laborers he had known at home with the slaves of Charleston, purely on the score of courtesy, of which he found the northern laborer "coarsely neglectful" and possibly even incapable. On this same southern trip he censoriously inserted in his journal the account of some "rude blackguards" laughing at President John Quincy Adams' bald pate as he swam in the Potomac.[14]

But for every instance of his distaste and distrust cropping out surreptitiously there are numerous examples in blunt form. As a young man he noted, "Aristocracy is a good sign . . . . 'Twere the greatest calamity to have it abolished." And he added, "No man would consent to live in society if he was obliged to admit everybody to his house that chose to come."[15] As he reached his thirties, he ruminated, "When were not the majority wicked?"[16] In his later thirties he recognized the superior individual not only as the root and seed of the ideal democracy but also as standing above most of society as he knew it: "Society in our bright hours seems not to claim equality, but ought to be treated like children to whom we administer camomile and magnesia on our own judgment, without consultation. What we can do is law enough for them."[17] In "Self-Reliance" he spoke of "the unintelligent brute force that lies at the bottom of society."[18] And apropos Thoreau's declaration of war, in his own way, with society, Emerson said, "A scholar has too humble an opinion of the population, of their possibilities, of their future, to be intitled to go to war with them as with equals."[19] And so it goes: Napoleon stands out from "the universal imbecility and indecision of men."[20] Webster, after the Compromise of 1850, "truly represents the American people just as they are, with their vast material interests, materialized intellect, and low morals."[21] And as an old man he was still saying it: "The people are to be taken in small doses."[22]

It is not surprising then to see a corollary distrust of the extension of suffrage. True to his intellectual heritage, Emerson is in favor of weighing heads, so to speak, rather than counting them, as comes out succinctly in his thoughts about George Bancroft's boast that the effective circulation of the Washington *Globe* was 300,000. "I ought to have said what utter nonsense to name in *my* ear this *number*, as if it were anything. Three million such people as can read the *Globe* with interest are as yet in too crude a state of nonage to deserve any regard."[23] Such persons obviously would fall outside the category of the "wise and robust," and freedom, said Emerson, "is dangerous and double-edged to any but the wise and robust."[24]

Everything up to this point leaves out of account Emerson's egalitarian sentiments. Though these are not as pervasive or as pungent in expression as the opposite sentiments, they are to be found in both word and action. While in residence at Cambridge in 1828 he inserted in his journal a typical bit of romantic primitivism: "I am always made uneasy when the conversation turns in my presence upon popular ignorance and the duty of adapting our public harangues and writings to the mind of the people. 'Tis all pedantry and ignorance. The people know as much and reason as well as we do. None so quick as they to discern brilliant genius or solid parts."[25] This was in July, and four months later "the people" elected Andrew Jackson. Possibly that is why we never find these particular sentiments repeated; but he was not yet ready to give over all romantic platitudes. He could still assert in 1845 that labor gave a certain nobility to the common man, made him "the bone and sinew of society," and made him more refreshing to the intellectual than the so-called "respectable elements."[26] In his domestic arrangements he attempted to be ultimately democratic by taking his maid and cook into the family circle at the table, only to be rebuffed by the cook's refusal.[27]

However, he was able at least once to resolve his opposing feelings. While granting the people's inability to recognize "genius or solid parts," and while feeling that "the people are to be taken in small doses," he was still able to find a certain degree of right-ness in their exercise of political power: "Let these rough riders—legislators in shirt-sleeves, Hossier, Sucker, Wolverine, Badger, or whatever hard head Arkansas, Oregon, or Utah sends, half orator, half assassin, to represent its wrath and cupidity in Washington—let these drive as they may, and the dispositions of territories and public lands, the necessities of balancing and keeping at bay the snarling majorities of German, Irish, and of native millions, will bestow promptness, address, and reason, at last, on our buffalo-hunter, and authority and majesty of manners. The instinct of the people is right."[28] This statement in 1860 is as near as Emer-son ever comes to a final resolution of his ambivalent feelings about the "people." His human sympathies were too broad for him to be a complacent Whig. But his intellectual and social heritage was too rich and too pervasive in his personality for him to hold a naive faith in *hoi polloi* or to mix easily with them. It is not an un-common dilemma for the intellectual.

II

Emerson's statement that the Whigs had the best men is gen-erally mirrored in his comments on political figures of the time. But again there is a certain ambivalence in his judgments.

He mentioned Jackson perhaps more than any other individual except Webster, and admiration and distaste are about equally divided. Uniformly, the basis for the first was Jackson's fine execu-tive energy—he was the epitome of self-reliance in the realm of action. But this admiration came late in Emerson's life, during the sixties. In "The Fortune of the Republic" he says, "How rare are acts of will! General Jackson was a man of will, and his phrase on one memorable occasion, 'I will take the responsibility,' is a proverb ever since."[29] On the other side of the ledger, but some twenty years earlier, we find Jackson deplored for essentially the same thing—his forceful personality. Or so it might appear. Actual-ly I think Emerson feared an unstable majority as much as he did a forceful leader when he said, "The Best are never demoniacal or magnetic, but all brutes are. The Democratic Party in this country is more magnetic than the Whig. Andrew Jackson is an eminent example of it."[30] Still earlier, during Jackson's first administration, he is decried for his *lack* of self-reliance, his subservience to the "bad party." Cromwell and Bonaparte, said Emerson, were thoroughly selfish, but at least they scorned servility, they were not the mob's slaves. Not so Jackson, for "If I want a favor of the President of the United States, I need not cultivate his personal kindness, I will go ask it of his President, the bad party in the country, and if they say yea, I shall be sure of Mr. Jackson's bow and smile and sign manual."[31] All this indicates that the older Emerson had a much broader view of Jackson's character than did the young Emerson; it also indicates that both his early censure and his later admiration grew out of the same antimajoritarian attitude, i.e., Jackson was admirable insofar as he threw off the shackles of party and asserted himself as a gifted individual. And he was bad insofar as he abdicated his own judgment and will, or, on other grounds, insofar as he used his personal magnetism to sway the majority toward an unworthy end.

Van Buren gets surprisingly little notice from Emerson, but none of it is favorable. Again the objection is on principle rather than on details, for Van Buren was another exponent of the numbers philosophy. Emerson apparently regarded him as the originator of the machine-politics system, because he recorded his distaste for the village political boss under the heading of "Van Burenism." "I saw the dictator of our rural Jacobins teaching his little circle of villagers their political lessons. And here, thought I, is one who loves what I hate."[32]

Emerson's attitudes toward certain famous Whigs are also significant. Perhaps the most famous New England Whig during Emerson's lifetime was Daniel Webster, and he was, understandably, one of young Emerson's heroes. His "earlier eloquence" in the Senate, Emerson recalled vividly when considering the possibility that the city of Washington might have to be abandoned during the Civil War.[33] But Emerson was aware fairly early of flaws in Webster's character. In 1843 he noted in his journal, "Any form of government would content me in which the rulers were gentlemen, but it is in vain that I have tried to persuade myself that Mr. Calhoun or Mr. Clay or Mr. Webster were such; they are underlings, and take the law from the dirtest fellows."[34] The Compromise of 1850 confirmed Emerson's growing suspicion of Webster's expediency, and in 1851 he saw Webster as representative of the low morals and materialized intellect of the American people, commenting "Webster's absence of moral faculty is degrading to the country."[35] In 1854 he was still pursuing this theme in his New York address on the Fugitive Slave Law.[36] His shift in attitude is most succinctly expressed by three verse fragments brought together by Edward Waldo Emerson in the Centenary Edition of his father's works under the heading "Webster." The first two, dated 1831 and 1834, are eulogistic of Webster's magnificent personal qualities; the third, dated 1854, a simple couplet:

Why did all manly gifts in Webster fail?
He wrote on Nature's grandest brow, *For Sale.*[37]

Whatever Webster's final position in history, it is unlikely that Emerson's simple view of him as a mercenary turncoat will have many adherents. Like Whittier's "Ichabod," Emerson's pronouncement at once partakes of and epitomizes the emotionally charged atmosphere of the time.

A Whig whom Emerson never ceased to admire was Horace Greeley. In 1851 he wrote, "I think Horace Greeley's career one of the most encouraging facts of our Whiggish age. A white-haired man in the city of New York has adopted every benevolent crotchet and maintained it until he commands an army of a million now in the heart of the United States."[38] The significance of this opinion will appear if we briefly examine Greeley's career.

In politics he was a protégé of Thurlow Weed, a thoroughgoing Whig and one of the ablest political organizers of his time. Warmhearted, impulsive, and motivated by a sincere humanitarian spirit, Greeley was nevertheless on all economic issues a true Whig. His great idol among politicians was Henry Clay, and he fought unceasingly for internal improvements, a high tariff, and the United States Bank; he opposed labor reforms with equal vehemence. His reputation as a radical and reformer came partly from his anti-slavery agitation, on which he entered not as a Democrat but as a "conscience" Whig, but mainly from his "feverish advocacy of side-show reforms"—such things as Fourierism, antitobacco, and antiliquor movements. And the first of these he supported because it was a road to utopia which did not require the change of the existing political structure: the Fourierists, in Greeley's view, could simply isolate themselves in their communities and forget about politics. But whatever his reforming crotchets, "his peculiarity in this respect," said Thurlow Weed, "never turned away from or impaired his consistent and hearty efforts in the Whig cause."[39]

This is the man whose career Emerson found "one of the most encouraging facts in our Whiggish age." What better illustration could there be of humanitarian sentiments overshadowing hard political facts than this idea of a Whig's Whig redeeming the "Whiggish age"?

In total view Emerson's political quandary is best described in terms of the tension between Emerson the man and Emerson the philosopher. In the latter role he could take the long view that culture of the individual was the only worthy end, that self-reliance and individualism and harmony of the individual with the moral universe were absolute values, and that it was both foolish and evil to lose sight of these values in concern for self and family or in reform of immediately pressing social ills. In this mood he saw that society would be good only when individuals were good, and that individual spirits are not reformed by party action. But as Mr. R. W. Emerson, *paterfamilias* and householder of Concord, Massachusetts, he was constantly being pulled back into the immediate world of pleasure and pain, of concern for his own, of good manners and bad manners, of demands upon his tender humanitarian feelings. If his responses to these demands sometimes appear inconsistent with his philosophy and unworthy of the philosopher, I think that few of us are in a position to throw stones at him. And, more important, to see Emerson in this perspective is to solve a good many puzzles about his writings and actions.

I would suggest, too, that Emerson's quandary is not his alone in his place and time. It would be the quandary of most New England intellectuals. The variety of solutions embraced by such men as Bancroft, Brownson, Bryant, Holmes, Whittier, Hawthorne, Thoreau, Frothingham, and Alcott indicates that finding a political home in this period was a complex process for most. Each man was probably driven by some impulses which he understood but dimly and controlled hardly at all, even though he may have held to a pretty thoroughly rationalized political position, as in the case of Bryant or Bancroft.

"Touching 'The Stylus' ":
Notes on Poe's Vision of Literary Order
by
Lewis P. Simpson

"Touching 'The Stylus':—this is the one great purpose of my literary life."—Edgar Poe to Philip Pendleton Cooke, 1846

LET US BEGIN somewhat indirectly by looking at two pictures. One is the daguerreotype portrait made of Edgar Poe during the autumn of 1848 at Providence, Rhode Island, where on November 15, 1848—if we can believe his own testimony—Poe attempted to end his life by taking an overdose of laudanum. In this representation Poe appears as a rather seedy gentleman, with his right hand thrust pretentiously into an untidy waistcoat. His haunted, unfocused stare indicates he may have been at the time drunk, doped, or as mad as Roderick Usher.[1] To say how many persons have been influenced in their conception of Poe by this daguerreotype would be impossible. But does it not resemble the dominant image in our memory of Poe more than any other depictions we have of him? It is the image of the demon-ridden "man apart" that Poe's Bohemian followers have made into a holy comforter of the alienated—the Poe to whom Baudelaire prayed and whom Mallarmé celebrated in his sonnet on Poe's tomb. Looked at in this way it symbolizes a dominant conviction of the modern literary temper, the alienation or isolation of the literary artist.

The other picture is a group picture which first came to my attention when I saw it used to illustrate a review of a collection of letters written by various authors to James T. Fields, successor to James Russell Lowell as editor of the *Atlantic Monthly*. Done

33

by a minor American painter, Thomas Hicks, it represents a large group of American writers whose careers spanned the first half of the nineteenth century. To us today, although probably not so much to people of the time, it seems grossly indiscriminate. Present are not only Cooper, Bryant, Irving, Emerson, Lowell, Holmes, Poe, Hawthorne, and Whittier (Thoreau, Melville, and Whitman are conspicuously absent) but also Mrs. Sedgwick, Mrs. Welby, Mrs. Sigourney, Mrs. Southworth, and others of that subliterary "d----d mob of scribbling women" that Hawthorne complained about. The general idea of the painting, however, is more interesting than the writers who appear in it. The setting is a classic rotunda. On either side are steps mounting to a spacious platform surrounded by columns crowned by Ionic capitals. In the center of this are three larger-than-life statues, representing, as I interpret them, Petrarch, the restorer of the classics, Homer (the central figure), the great original poet, and Dante, the hero of the vernacular tongues. In their Olympian tranquillity these literary immortals gaze out over the American authors, who are depicted in various seated and standing postures on the flanking staircases and in the area below. Thus the writers of the new nation are viewed in an idealized relationship to the Western literary tradition, and the painting manages to suggest, if somewhat ludicrously, the continuity, authority, fraternity, and not least, the public importance and dignity of the literary life.[2] We see in it a symbolic representation of a literary spirit belonging more to another age than to ours, the spirit of literary community.

Now, Poe, many of us would be inclined to say, does not belong in this second picture at all; the image of him is so strongly that of the alienated artist. Interestingly enough, Thomas Hicks seems to have had some reservations about Poe's place in the American literary community. He depicts him wearing a black cloak, standing with his back to Hawthorne and gazing downward, withdrawn and introverted.[3] Is Hicks merely presenting the romantic poet of popular legend, or is he trying to convey a sense of a special relationship Poe had to the world of letters, to say in effect that Poe was both of the public brotherhood of writers and not of it? Probably not, but the question is worth asking. It can, I think, be made the basis for a study of Poe's whole literary career as a quest for literary order. In the present essay my purpose is more modest. I should like only to offer some speculative notes—and I should like to emphasize that my remarks are intended to be speculative—on the significance of Poe's long-continued, abortive efforts to establish his own literary magazine, which he first called the *Penn Magazine* and later the *Stylus*.

I

The *Stylus*, it seems to me, was Poe's chief attempt to realize a vision of establishing literary order in the United States. To be sure, the personal motives in Poe's desire to have his own magazine must be readily admitted. Poe knew the literary situation of his day not as a dispassionate observer but as a desperately involved participant; and the aspirations which prompted his literary adventures were always intensely personal. In fact, the story of the *Stylus* can be read simply as the history of a frustrated private ambition that persisted beyond possibility of realization into illusion and finally into hallucination. But Poe's fruitless endeavors to publish the *Stylus* should be viewed in a broader context than that of his individual literary ambition. When this context is developed, Poe's motives, we realize, were more than personal, his failure more than personal.

In its broadest context Poe's dream of the *Stylus* is properly not less than what may well be regarded as the major phenomenon of the literary history of the Western world during the past century and a half: the decline of the kind of sensibility (to use an overworked but useful term) we see in Hicks's painting, the sensibility of literary community. The more limited context of the *Stylus* was the expression of this decline in the United States following the Jacksonian revolution.

Although its origins may be traced into antiquity and even into Old Testament times, the sensibility of literary community, which cannot be explored here beyond a few generalities, was first clearly present in the three orders of the ecumenical Christian Republic: the *sacerdotium*, the *imperium*, and the *studium*. With the coming of humanism and the rise of secularism, the boundaries

of the *studium*, the realm of letters and learning as distinguished
from the realms of church and state, widened beyond its first pre-
cinct, the cosmopolitan medieval universities. There emerged in
humanist minds the image of a secular European literary and intellectual order, an ideal polity of the mind commonly called the
"Republic of Letters" or the "Commonwealth of Letters" or perhaps the "Republic (or Commonwealth) of Letters and Learning." To document the existence of this symbolic community in
the European imagination is not difficult; references to it are
omnipresent, and it is still defined in one way or another in all
modern dictionaries.[4] To assess its significance, however, is extremely hard; for like any generalization about class, nation, or
tradition, it defies pragmatic study. It was, and is in the attenuated
existence it has today, a rough metaphysical construct expressing
faith in the capacity of the scholarly and critical humane mind to
create and maintain its own dominion through the fraternity
and discipline of letters. "Skill in letters" was still, as in the Middle Ages when grammar was the first of the seven liberal arts, the
basis of all education and of all educated communication. (Until
the nineteenth century, it is useful to recall, "letters" and "learning" were synonymous, as were the terms "literature" and "science.") The sensibility of the Republic of Letters reached its
greatest power in the eighteenth century, when it seemed to Voltaire, for example, that the literary republic had become a genuine
reality. Taking stock of the European intellectual situation in the
middle of that century, Voltaire wrote: "We have seen impercepti-
bly established in Europe, in spite of wars and religious differences,
a literary republic. All the sciences, all the arts have thus received
mutual aid. . . . True scholars in each field have strengthened this
great society of minds, reaching everywhere and everywhere independent."[5] In Voltaire's opinion the numerous academies which
had sprung up in Europe constituted this republic. But the spirit
of the Republic of Letters found expression wherever men of letters congregated in the literary capitals of Europe—in taverns, coffee houses, salons, and printing houses. From Edinburgh, to Paris,
to St. Petersburg the man of letters—and this comprehensive designation covered not only the historian, teacher, novelist, poet, es-
sayist, and editor, but the statesman, lawyer, and physician as well

—assumed his citizenship in the literary order. The Republic of Letters was the controlling image of the intellectual and literary organization of Europe, the symbolic public dominion (*respublica literarum*) of the humane mind.

Of course any man of letters in a pragmatic mood could readily point to the discrepancies between actual literary existence and the ideal existence. The Republic of Letters, Oliver Goldsmith once said, should be called "an anarchy of literature."[6] But this kind of hardheaded realism did not disturb the image of the literary republic appreciably. What did disturb it increasingly from the late eighteenth century on were revolutionary forces tending toward the intellectual and spiritual chaos of the present century. Among these, to oversimplify considerably, we may single out integral nationalism, which would identify the life of the mind with that of the particular nation; antiurban, anti-institutional Rousseauistic primitivism, which would locate man in a new relation to nature; equalitarian education, which would render the crucial distinction between the man of letters and the man of no letters meaningless; highly exploitative industrial capitalism, which would make intellectual creation product and commodity; and modern science and technology, which would split the intellect into fragments, separate letters from learning, and eventually greatly reduce the importance of words in communication. The time was coming when such notions as the solidarity of men of letters and the unifying function of the literary discipline would cease to be cultural axioms. With the waning of the appeal of the Republic of Letters, symbols of the estrangement of the literary existence from society would come into being.

By the mid-nineteenth century the most dramatic of these had been conceived in the transformation of the image of the man of letters into the image of the isolated artist. This image idealized the writer who, believing his values and those of society to be completely opposed, became a dedicated minority of one. In fact, though, this symbol of isolation, which we can see emerging from Shelley's *Defence of Poetry* onward, was less appealing than another new symbol of the literary life, that commonly called "Bohemia." In this symbol the feeling for literary community found renewed and more intense expression. Bohemia—we have to distinguish the real Bohemia from the fake Bohemia—was a special development out of the old sensibility of the Republic of Letters. It continued the assumption of the fraternity and authority of the literary life and the obligation of the writer to the literary realm. The rise of the sensibility of alienation, in other words, was relative to the persistence of the sensibility of literary community in European society. Letters and learning continued to exist in the image of a public realm. Perhaps this is why even such a disaffected writer as Baudelaire stood for election to the French Academy.[7]

To a discernible degree, then, in Europe the growing tendency to literary isolationsim was assimilated by the traditional sensibility of the Republic of Letters. In the United States a different literary situation existed. If through some unhistorical trickery, history had operated in this country at the sluggish pace Thomas Jefferson believed it would—a thousand generations would pass before the full occupation of the continent, he said at the beginning of the nineteenth century—our literary history might well have been different. For the patrician mind which Jefferson represented and which dominated the culture of the early American Republic had a distinct regard for the European conviction of the realm of letters. The writings of Benjamin Franklin, John Adams, and others, as well as those of Jefferson, attest to this. But following the Jacksonian revolution the new nation more and more identified the aims of its existence with the insurgent forces threatening the sensibility of literary community in Western civilization. This indeed was America's historical destiny, since this nation was born at the moment when nationalism, democracy, capitalism, and technology began definitively to shape the course of the future. The aspiration to create a unique national literature, the desire to vest literary authority in the masses of the recently literate, the tendency to elevate political, economic, and mechanical pursuits above contemplative ones—these characteristics of American thought were rooted in the *Zeitgeist* of the nineteenth century. In dynamic, frontier-oriented America, however, they operated more unrestrainedly than in Europe. The result was that the decline of the directing, assimilating sense of the Republic of Letters was more rapid in America than in Europe. The American literary situation became increasingly anomalous.

In only one place in the United States did the old assumption of the solidarity of literature and the literary life persist to any marked degree. This was in New England, or a small part of New England, the Boston region, where Boston, Cambridge (or Harvard University), and Concord made up a literary community. Existing for the nation in the image of Boston, the "American Athens," home of the *North American Review*, the Boston Athenaeum, and the Saturday Club, the city of Lowell, Holmes, Longfellow, and the later Emerson, this community of letters symbolized the fading idealism of the Republic of Letters. To the literati whom it accepted, and who accepted it, it afforded a sense of belonging to the literary realm. Those who stood apart, notably Thoreau, were hardly Bohemians of the European variety, but like the European writers their sense of alienation was tempered by their feeling for the social dominion of letters. James Russell Lowell's well-known essay on Thoreau attacks him bitterly for lacking "that generosity of 'communication' which Johnson admired in Burke."[8] Lowell might well have pondered the sense of the community, or communion, of letters which Thoreau expresses in the chapter on "Reading" in *Walden*.

II

Since Poe was unable to accept Boston any more than Boston was able to accept him, the possibility of his identifying himself with the only coherent literary culture in America was nullified early in his career. Instead he participated more intimately and more constantly in the life of America's Grub Street—Grub Street must not be confused with Bohemia—than any other major American writer of the nineteenth century. As a literary contributor, editor, and critic he was particularly involved in the New York version of Grub Street, probably in the mid-nineteenth century the grubbiest Grub Street in the world, a "literary butcher shop" Perry Miller calls it.[9] In this world of quackery Poe was fully exposed to the loss of the guiding idealism of literary community.

His intense desire to impose order on the disorder of the American literary situation is a discernible motive in his *Marginalia*, in his *Literati of New York City*, and in his proposed broader work, *Literary America*. The center of his vision of literary order was always his ideal magazine, which he declared to be "the one great purpose of my literary life."

Exactly when the story of the *Stylus* begins, it is impossible to say on the basis of documentary evidence. Poe must have begun to dream of having his own magazine in the earliest days of his literary career. And after he left his first editorial post with the *Southern Literary Messenger* in 1837, his ambition to establish and control a magazine undoubtedly acquired a central importance in his plans. The first definite mention of the never-to-be-realized magazine occurs two years later, when we find him remarking to Philip Pendleton Cooke, "As soon as Fate allows I will have a Magazine of my own."[10] In a few more months he was boldly courting Fate by issuing in the Philadelphia *Saturday Courier* a "Prospectus of the Penn Magazine, a Monthly Literary Journal, to be Edited and Published in the City of Philadelphia, By Edgar A. Poe." Because this is the chief document in the history of Poe's illusory magazine, I will quote from it at some length:

> To those who remember the early days of the Southern periodical in question [the *Southern Literary Messenger*] it will be scarcely necessary to say that its main feature was a somewhat overdone causticity in its department of Critical Notices of new books. The Penn Magazine will retain this trait of severity in so much only as the calmest yet sternest sense of justice will permit. Some years since elapsed may have mellowed down the petulance without interfering with the rigour of the critic. Most surely they have not taught him to read through the medium of a publisher's will, nor convinced him that the interests of letters are unallied with the interests of truth. It shall be the first and chief purpose of the Magazine now proposed to become known as one where may be found at all times, and upon all subjects, an honest and a fearless opinion. It shall be a leading object to assert in precept, and to maintain in practice the rights, while in effect it demonstrates the advantages, of an absolutely independent criticism—a criticism self-sustained; guiding itself only by the purest rules of Art, analyzing and urging these rules as

it applies them; holding itself aloof from all personal bias; acknowledging no fear save that of outraging the right, yielding no point either to the vanity of the author, or to the assumptions of antique prejudice, or to the involute and anonymous cant of the Quarterlies, or to the arrogance of those organized *cliques* which, hanging like nightmares upon American literature, manufacture, at the nod of our principal booksellers, a pseudo-public opinion by wholesale. These are objects of which no man may need be ashamed. They are purposes, moreover, whose novelty at least will give them interest. For assurance that I will fulfill them in the best spirit and to the very letter, I appeal with confidence to the many thousands of my friends, who sustained me in the Messenger, where I had but a very partial opportunity of completing my own plans.

In respect to the other features of the Penn Magazine, a few words here will suffice. It will endeavour to support the general interests of the republic of letters, without reference to particular regions; regarding the world at large as the true audience of the author. Beyond the precincts of literature, properly so called, it will leave in better hands the task of instruction upon all matters of *very* grave moment. Its aim chiefly shall be to *please*; and this through means of versatility, originality, and pungency. It may be as well here to observe that nothing said in this Prospectus should be construed into a design of sullying the Magazine with any tincture of the buffoonery, scurrility, or profanity, which are the blemish of some of the most vigorous of the European prints. In all branches of the literary department, the best aid, from the highest and purest sources, is secured.[11]

Norman Foerster calls this prospectus the best statement Poe made of his "ideal in criticism." But its chief significance, I conjecture, lies in the implications of the divided purposes Poe pledges his magazine to. In the first place, Poe declares his magazine will devote itself to "an absolutely independent criticism; a criticism self-sustained; guiding itself only by the purest rules of Art." In the second place, he asserts it will "support the general interests of the republic of letters, without reference to particular regions; regarding the world at large as the true audience of the author." At first glance we do not see much if any discrepancy between these intentions; in a closer study of Poe's prospectus we uncover a fundamental discrepancy.

James Russell Lowell, who was familiar with Poe's magazine project, says in his essay on Poe, "Had Mr. Poe had the control of a magazine of his own, in which to display his critical abilities, he would have been as autocratic, ere this, in America, as Professor Wilson has been in England; and his criticisms, we are sure, would have been far more profound and philosophical than those of the Scotsman."[12] Lowell's image of Poe as an American version of John Wilson, the noted critic of *Blackwood's Magazine*, was unquestionably appealing to Poe, who clearly in his criticism essayed the role of the literary autocrat or dictator in the tradition descending through such figures as Ben Jonson, John Dryden, Alexander Pope, and Samuel Johnson. This tradition was an integral part of the lore and legend of the Republic of Letters. Yet in the prospectus of the *Penn*, the implied image of the man of letters playing the role of arbiter in the world of letters is subordinated to a more strongly implied image, which is not that of a human arbiter at all but that of a "criticism self-sustained." We are reminded of Allen Tate's remark that no writer in the United States, England, or France during the nineteenth century went so far in "his vision of dehumanized man" as Poe.[13] Tate is showing how Poe's view of the cosmic destiny of man in *Eureka* is an extension of his vision of the ordering of human existence through sheer mechanical sensation and will. His vision of literary order in the statement about the *Penn* is likewise an extension of his vision of dehumanized man. As such it can be related to the total complex of motives which drove Poe to reject life in favor of death.

This goes beyond my intention. I want simply to suggest that in his vision of bringing literary order to the incoherent, corrupt literary situation in the United States, Poe creates an almost complete split between alienation and community. Essentially he posits two symbolic literary realms. There is, Poe fails to realize, no easy nor even necessary relation between the two. The distance between his absolutely autonomous, depersonalized if not dehumanized, realm of Pure Art and the traditional public dominion of letters is far greater than the distance between Bohemia and the Republic of Letters. In fact, the sensibility controlling Poe's realm of Pure Art is not different in degree but different in kind from that governing the literary republic. The two realms are discontinuous.

This does not exhaust the unresolved conflicts in Poe's vision of literary order. A further complication is introduced when we consider his inclination to accept the spirit and techniques of nineteenth-century journalism. This is implied in the prospectus of the *Penn* and emerges plainly in a series of almost identical letters Poe wrote to prominent American men of letters, including Washington Irving, John Pendleton Kennedy, Henry Wadsworth Longfellow, and Fitz-Greene Halleck, on behalf of the *Penn*. An extract from the letter to Irving will suffice for illustration:

> I need not call you [*sic*] attention to the signs of the times in respect to Magazine literature. You will admit the tendency of the age in this direction. The brief, the terse, the condensed, and the easily circulated will take the place of the diffuse, the ponderous, and inaccessible. Even our reviews are found too massive for the taste of the day—I do not mean for the taste of the merely uneducated, but also for that of the few. In the meantime the finest minds of Europe are beginning to lend their spirit to Magazines. In this country, unhappily, we have not any journal of the class, which either can afford to offer pecuniary inducements to the highest talent, or which would be, in all respects, a fitting vehicle for its thoughts. In the supply of this deficiency there would be a point gained; and the project of which I speak has originated in the hope of supplying it.[14].

In the *Marginalia* Poe makes the same point more explicitly:

> The increase, within a few years, of the magazine literature, is by no means to be regarded as indicating what some critics would suppose it to indicate—a downward tendency in American taste or letters. It is but a sign of the times, an indication of an era in which men are forced upon the curt, the condensed, the well-digested in place of the voluminous—in a word, upon journalism in lieu of dissertation. We need now the light artillery rather than the peace-makers of the intellect. I will not be sure that men at present think more profoundly than half a century ago, but beyond question they think with more rapidity, with more skill, with more tact, with more of method and less of excresence in the thought. Besides all this, they have a vast

increase in the thinking material; they have more facts, more to think about. For this reason, they are disposed to put the greatest amount of thought in the smallest compass and disperse it with the utmost attainable rapidity. Hence the journalism of the age; hence, in especial, magazines.[15]

Apparently Poe, who liked to call himself a "magazinist," had glimpses of creating a literary dominion in America different from either the transcendent realm of Pure Art or the comprehensive Republic of Letters. Both of these assume leisure. Poe was drawn toward a pragmatic compromise with the dynamic "time spirit" of the New World, where the present threatened to overwhelm not only the past but the eternal as well. At least he was so drawn in certain moods. He would never have joined those who, like Cornelius Matthews and other "Young Americans," were seeking virtually to isolate American letters in the humming present.

III

If Poe's vision of directing and organizing American letters was divided, it was based on a central assumption: namely, the necessity of literary order. His vain and torturous efforts for a decade to see his ideal magazine into print illustrate graphically the irony of such an assumption in the literary environment in which he existed.

The date of the first issue of the *Penn* was supposed to be January, 1841. When this date came around, Poe announced publication would be delayed until March, 1841. By the end of this month he was writing to his friend Dr. J. E. Snodgrass: "The Penn, I hope, is only 'scotched, not killed.' It would have appeared under glorious auspices, and with capital at command, in March, as advertised, but for the unexpected bank suspensions."[16] Whether Poe's explanation of the failure of the *Penn* to materialize is correct or not is uncertain. Likely he considerably exaggerated the extent of the backing he had for it. In any event he suspended his project while he went back to editing a magazine for someone else, in this case the owner of *Graham's Magazine*.

In January, 1843, after changing the punning title of his proposed magazine from the *Penn Magazine* to a deeply symbolic one, the *Stylus*, Poe entered into an agreement with Thomas C. Clarke, a Philadelphia publisher, to bring out his long-delayed periodical. A prospectus was issued and Poe sketched a title page for the *Stylus*. This second prospectus which Poe wrote for his ideal magazine places a greater emphasis on the Republic of Letters than the first one:

> The new journal will endeavor to be at the same time more varied and more unique;—more vigorous, more pungent, more original, more individual, and more independent. It will discuss not only the Belles-Lettres, but, very thoroughly, the Fine Arts, with the Drama; and, more in brief, will give, each month, a Retrospect of our Political History. It will enlist the loftiest talent, but employ it not always in the loftiest—at least not always in the most pompous or Puritanical way. It will aim at affording a fair and not dishonorable field for the *true* intellect of the land, without reference to the mere prestige of celebrated names. It will support the general interests of the Republic of Letters, and insist upon regarding the world at large as the sole proper audience for the author. It will resist the dictation of Foreign Reviews. It will eschew the stilted dulness of our own Quarterlies, and while it *may*, if necessary, be no less learned, will deem it wiser to be less anonymous and difficult to be more dishonest, than they.[17]

The general tone of this is about the same as that in the earlier prospectus, but, we note, Poe announces a greater variety of subject matter for the *Stylus* and does not insist upon the limitation to "literature, properly so called." Consequently, he is more in harmony with the traditional image of the Republic of Letters. Yet Poe concludes the second prospectus, as he commenced the first one, with a firm appeal to "a criticism self-sustained; guiding itself only by the purest rules of Art." Thus the second statement reveals more sharply than the first the split in Poe's literary sensibility between alienation and community.[18]

Again fate blocked Poe's magazine. It did not come into being even briefly, as had James Russell Lowell's *Pioneer* the same year. By June, 1843—the *Stylus* was scheduled to make its debut in July, 1843—Poe was writing to Lowell: "I received your poem, which you undervalue, and which I think truly beautiful—as, indeed, I do all you have ever written—but alas! my Magazine scheme has exploded—or, at least, I have been deprived, through the imbecility, or rather through the idiocy of my partner, of all means of prosecuting it for the present. Under better auspices I may resume it next year."[19]

Although feasible "auspices" did not appear again, Poe never ceased to seek them. The next year he wrote to Lowell, who had cooled toward him, suggesting "that the elite of our men of letters should combine secretly" and each subscribe two hundred dollars to establish a monthly literary magazine. No reply came from Lowell. Poe figured some more and wrote to Lowell again a few months later, urging that twelve "influential men of letters" form a corporation to get out a magazine, each one buying a share of stock at one hundred dollars. The results would be salutary: "The works should be printed in the very best manner, and should address the aristocracy of talent. We might safely give, for $5, a pamphlet of 128 pp. and, with the support of the variety of our personal influence, we might easily extend the circulation to 20,000 —giving $100,000. The expenses would not exceed $40,000—if indeed reach 20,000 when the work should be fairly established. Thus there would be $60,000 to be divided among 12—$5000 per an:apiece."[20] The plan was not entirely fantastic; but Poe by now was beginning to sound like the tracts being issued by the multifarious tribe of American schemers and promoters.

Month after month, year after year went by. Poe followed his vision into illusion, and eventually into hallucination. In 1846 we find him, following the demise of the *Broadway Journal*, with which he had been associated, writing to Sarah J. Hale: "The B. Journal had fulfilled its destiny—which was a matter of no great moment. I have never regarded it as more than a temporary adjunct to other designs. I am now busy making arrangement for the establishment of a Magazine which offers a wide field for literary ambition. Professor Chas. Anthon has agreed to take charge for me of a Department of Criticism on Scholastic Letters. His name will be announced. I shall have, also, a Berlin and a Parisian correspondent—both of eminence. The first No. may not appear until Jan. 1847."[21] Professor Charles Anthon, an acquaintance of

Poe, might conceivably have agreed to work with him. The Berlin and Paris correspondents were almost surely fictitious, though they may have been real enough to Poe. January, 1847, came and went. The *Stylus* did not appear.

Finally, in the last year of his life, Poe once again saw "auspices," this time in the person of one Edward H. N. Patterson of the semi-frontier community of Oquawka, or Yellow Banks, located on the Mississippi River in Illinois. Here the story becomes ludicrous, for Patterson, it seems, wanted to publish the *Stylus* in Oquawka, an impractical, not to say ironic, location from which to consider "the general interests of the Republic of Letters," not to mention those of Pure Art. But Poe seemingly was willing to try St. Louis, if he could not get Patterson to agree to New York, and, still confident that he could muster 20,000 subscribers for the magazine, told Patterson that he proposed

> to take a tour through the principal States—especially West & South—visiting the small towns more particularly than the large ones—lecturing as I went, to pay expenses—and staying sufficiently long in each place to interest my personal friends (old College & West Point acquaintances scattered all over the land) in the success of the enterprize. By these means, I would guarantee, in 3 months (or 4) to get 1000 subs. in advance, with their signatures—nearly all pledged to pay on the issue of the first number. Under such circumstances, success would be certain. I have now about 200 names pledged to support me whenever I venture on the undertaking—which perhaps you are aware I have long had in contemplation—only awaiting a *secure* opportunity.[22]

Negotiations continued with Patterson, who held out for a three-dollar instead of a five-dollar magazine. "The mere idea of a '$3 Magazine' would suggest namby-pamby-ism & frivolity," Poe exclaimed indignantly to his potential sponsor, who agreed to the five-dollar magazine if Poe could raise a thousand subscribers.[23] An arrangement was made for Poe to meet Patterson in St. Louis during October, 1849. Poe planned, lectured to try to raise money to get to St. Louis, although he likely never really meant to go, and continued to drink. He died in Baltimore on October 7, 1849. A few months before he had written to George W. Eveleth:

"Touching 'The Stylus': . . . I am awaiting the *best opportunity* for its issue—and if by waiting until the day of judgment I perceive still increasing chances of ultimate success, why until the day of judgment I will patiently wait."[24] Now his patience would no longer be strained by mortal anxieties.

IV

If through some combination of fortuitous circumstances, Poe had actually managed to publish the *Stylus* for a decade, would it have influenced the course of American literary history to any extent? Would it have become, as Poe dreamed it would, an organizing locus, an intellectual capital, of American letters? Even if we grant Poe more tempermental stability as an editor and man of letters than he seems to have had, this is doubtful. His ambiguous juxtaposition of the Republic of Letters, the realm of Pure Art, and the realm of Journalism in his vision of literary order is symptomatic of an intangible yet definite truth: the culture in which Poe lived did not, by and large, believe in the existence of the realm of letters. By his time the decline of the sensibility of literary community had proceeded too far in America.

Poe's vision of literary order and the abortive story of the *Stylus*, we can see from our perspective today, serve to help document the history of a lost cause, that of bringing literary order to the anomalous condition of American letters. Although it is a lost cause and has always been a lost cause, it has never been abandoned. Indeed the major significance of Poe's vision may well be the way in which his concept of a "criticism self-sustained" anticipates the strenuous, prescriptive, some say Alexandrian, domain of the so-called "New Criticism," which at times has made impossible demands not only of art but of criticism itself.[25]

A New Reading of Melville's "Benito Cereno"

by
Nicholas Canaday, Jr.

CRITICAL INTERPRETATIONS OF Herman Melville's "Benito Cereno" have hitherto sought to explore its meaning in terms of good and evil. From such an approach problems have arisen because of the apparent vagueness and inconsistency of controlling symbols, because of an uncertainty as to Melville's stand on slavery as an institution, and because of the story's conclusion in the form of a legal deposition.[1] Another reading of "Benito Cereno," which views the theme of authority as this tale's organizing principle, or the structural framework on which is displayed a proliferation of ideas, may resolve these difficulties and justify its parts on artistic and thematic grounds. The theme of a ship captain's authority is not unfamiliar to readers of Melville's novels dealing with the sea.[2]

"Benito Cereno," an account of the results of a successful mutiny by Negroes aboard a Spanish slave ship in 1799, pictures the un-usual situation that results when a captain is held as a prisoner aboard his own ship for a period of about three months. When at last an American captain boards the hapless slaver in an isolated harbor off the southern coast of Chile, this outsider views with amazement the ambiguous status of Captain Benito Cereno, who wears the uniform and carries the sword of authority but seems to have lost command of his ship. The American sealer, *Bachelor's Delight*, has put into the lonely harbor for the purpose of replenishing its water casks. Early in the morning of the second day in

49

the harbor, the American captain, Amasa Delano, sees the strange ship entering the bay. He recognizes it as a Spanish merchantman, but he cannot fail to notice its tattered state of disrepair and that its master narrowly misses running it aground in the harbor. Believing that the Spaniard may have been the victim of a storm at sea or of an epidemic of disease among the crew, Captain Delano boards the ship to offer his aid to its captain. Once aboard the ship, which is named the *San Dominick*, he finds the decks and rigging in a state of complete disorder. The captain with a few Spanish sailors exercises a very uncertain discipline over a large group of Negroes. Don Benito confirms the American's idea that misfortune has overtaken the ship, but the Spanish captain is reluctant to supply any details. His vagueness and evasiveness puzzle the American, but the Spaniard's appearance, an aristocratic bearing weakened by suffering, casts out the suspicions of the American while arousing his pity. Don Benito is so weak that he never leaves the arm of his Negro body servant, Babo, and never gives his orders to the crew except through him. The inefficacy of these orders is repeatedly observed by Amasa Delano during his stay of a few hours aboard the *San Dominick*, but he agrees to supply the Spanish ship with needed provisions and sailcloth. It is only when Captain Delano is leaving the *San Dominick* and Don Benito jumps desperately into his parting boat that the American realizes the truth about the situation. The Negroes under the leadership of Babo had revolted against their captain, killing all the Spanish officers except Benito Cereno and reducing him to the status of a slave. After escaping from the slaver with its captain, Delano sends his American crew to recapture the *San Dominick* from the Negro mutineers. The assault by the Americans is successful, and the Negroes who survive are captured and turned over to a Spanish court in Peru, where they are tried for mutiny, convicted, and executed.

The elements providing for the theme of authority in "Benito Cereno" fall into several categories. The first is the action itself, a mutiny at sea, which must necessarily entail a revolt against authority.[3] Since the tradition of seafaring men has always recognized the grave seriousness of such a revolt, a captain is granted extraordinary authority while at sea. Melville reinforces the basic situation of mutiny at sea by using specific symbols to indicate that a loss of command has occurred aboard the Spanish ship. Melville's technique in telling the story affords the reader a double view of Don Benito's position as a captain. The beginning of the tale is told from the point of view of the American captain, who is totally unaware at first that there has been a mutiny aboard the stricken ship. When the facts are later revealed, the story is recounted through the second medium of the court records concerning the mutiny, and the concept of authority is examined from a second point of view.

Even from a distance Captain Delano shows his astonishment at the incompetency of the *San Dominick*'s master, if not at his lack of authority. Loss of command to some degree is indicated when the Spanish ship sails into St. Maria harbor in disreputable condition, flying no colors, and barely misses a sunken reef as it navigates the entrance to the bay. The name of the ship bears connotations of domination and command, but the gilt letters spelling it out on the ship's headboards are tarnished and faded, "each letter streakingly corroded."[4] Not only is the *San Dominick*'s name scarcely visible on its hull because of corrosion, but also the letters are obscured because "like mourning weeds, dark festoons of sea grass slimily swept to and fro over the name, with every hearse-like roll of the hull" (70). Melville's words here point to the presence of death aboard the ship as well as to a loss of command. More clearly visible than the name of the ship is a motto chalked along the forward side: "Seguid vuestro jefe" (Follow your leader). The motto refers to the skeleton of the slaves' former master, which has been nailed to the ship's prow but is concealed by a canvas at the approach of the American captain. The words have been improvised by the Negroes as a threat to enforce the obedience of the Spanish sailors still left alive. Ironically, the motto also represents a perversion of command: no domineering ship captain rules the *San Dominick*, but a savage "leader" cruelly oppressive toward his victims. The ship's stern piece, an intricately carved symbolical device, "uppermost and central of which was a dark satyr in a mask, holding his foot on the prostrate neck of a writhing figure, likewise masked" (70), combines elements of both mystery and tyranny. It depicts the same tyrannical control that is suggested by the name of the ship and the chalked motto, but the masks provide for a reversal in the role of tyrant and subject not envisioned by the ship fitters of Castile.

Once aboard the ship, Captain Delano finds his impressions of disorder dismally strengthened. Negroes shuffle idly about the deck bent on no specific tasks, the confusion he had perceived at a distance is confirmed, and six Negroes sit in a row on the elevated poop of the quarterdeck polishing and clashing hatchets. Even a landsman would recognize the usurpation of authority indicated by such a gang on the quarter-deck, the traditional podium from which a captain speaks his commands.

His meeting with the vessel's captain increases Delano's vague apprehension. Don Benito's outward and inward appearances are at odds. Melville contrasts the "singular richness" of his costume with the "dreary, spiritless look" in his eyes (73). That he wears only the outward shell of authority is not apparent to Captain Delano, and yet the disorder aboard the ship and Don Benito's uneasiness are enough to motivate the American captain to speculate on the entire situation. These speculations are concerned with the nature of a captain's authority aboard a ship, but they are based upon the premise that Benito Cereno is indeed in command of the *San Dominick*. Although this assumption is false, it affords Melville the opportunity to examine certain aspects of a captain's authority under normal conditions. It is Captain Delano's conclusion that storms at sea, scarcity of water and provisions, and injuries and sickness among the crew—in short, a long-continued period of suffering has acted to impair the authority of the captain over his crew. Melville confirms this line of reasoning: "But, under the circumstances, precisely this condition of things was to have been anticipated. In armies, navies, cities, or families, in nature herself, nothing more relaxes good order than misery" (74). Since relaxing of good order because of external circumstances does not necessarily mean the destruction of authority if the ship's captain maintains command by the vigor of his character and the strength of his physical stature, Captain Delano then goes on to observe the physical debility of the Spaniard. The American captain believes that an energetic leader would have overcome such difficulties as have beset the Spanish ship, and by his personal

actions would have reinforced his challenged authority and prevented such misrule. Physically, Don Benito is described as a sick
man, "suddenly pausing, starting, or staring, biting his lip, biting
his finger-nail, flushing, paling, twitching his beard, with other
symbols of an absent or moody mind" (74). Melville stresses the
fact that the Spaniard's voice (an obvious symbol of command)
has been reduced to a hoarse and husky whisper. The physical
condition of Don Benito appears to Captain Delano to be the result of a long-standing pulmonary complaint. Melville interjects
no comment on this conclusion, since it will later become apparent
that the Spanish captain's ineffectualness is not fundamentally
physical in its source. Yet because of Delano's mistaken assumption, Melville has the opportunity to indicate how important he
considers a vigorous physical presence, stature, and power as ad-
juncts to authority.[5]

Another element observed by Captain Delano in Don Benito's
demeanor is his reserve in exercising authority. That he shows
distinct aversion to every contact with the Negroes is believed by
Delano to stem from some mental disorder accompanying his physical debility, although the American admits the possibility that
this reserve may proceed from design. This latter speculation permits Melville to discourse upon the general policy of ship com-
manders to remain aloof from the men in their charge, that "icy
though conscientious policy, more or less adopted by all com-
manders of large ships, which, except in signal emergencies, oblit-
erates alike the manifestations of sway with every trace of sociality"
(77). Melville recognizes here one of the first principles of main-
taining authority, a principle which demands that a person in
command avoid undue familiarity with his subordinates.[6]

After his conversation with the ship's master, Captain Delano
retires in solitude to await the return of his boat and to reflect upon
the curious incidents which have occurred. He has observed four
breaches of discipline that have a bearing on Don Benito's authority or the lack of it. On the one hand, during their conversation Don Benito had ignored the knifing of a Spanish sailor and
the trampling of another by the Negroes; on the other hand, the
Spanish captain had tyrannized over a black slave in chains and
drawn cringing submission from many of the other Negroes in the

mob amidships. To Captain Delano, who is unaware that the two
latter incidents are a part of the mutineers' plot to hoodwink him,
the events seem contradictory. He decides that Benito Cereno is a
weak and capricious commander, and he remarks: "I know no
sadder sight than a commander who has little of command but
the name" (85). This statement is the literal truth about the
Spaniard, but as yet Captain Delano has not perceived its full implications.

The qualities in Captain Delano that show the ease with which
he maintains his own command make possible his mistaken notion
about the state of affairs aboard the *San Dominick*. Melville's
initial view of Don Benito's loss of authority is through the eyes of
Captain Delano, and thus it is a view that ostensibly does not take
into account the fact that a mutiny has occurred. That the American captain's mistake is not only credible but indeed natural and
inevitable is assured by Melville's presentation of the character
of Amasa Delano. He is accustomed to instant and exact obedience
to his own commands. This dominance is illustrated by the action
of his own crew throughout the narrative, especially by the hearty
alacrity with which they undertake the dangerous mission of re-
capturing the *San Dominick*. It is the nature of Delano's authority,
accepted without question by his men and assumed automatically
by himself, that makes it impossible for him to imagine a captain
aboard a ship who does not exercise the same sway. As if this were
not enough to ensure credibility in his adventure, Melville carefully discloses an important trait of his character in the beginning
of the narrative when Delano first sights the disheveled *San Dominick* sailing into the harbor without a flag. The American has
heard of lawlessness occurring in such lonely spots, but he is merely surprised by the approach of the strange ship, not in the least
distrustful. This surprise does not turn into uneasiness because,
according to Melville, he is "a person of singularly undistrustful
good nature, not liable, except on extraordinary and repeated in-
centives, and hardly then, to indulge in personal alarms, any way
involving the imputation of malign evil in man" (67). To this
analysis Melville adds the ambiguous remark: "Whether, in view
of what humanity is capable, such a trait implies, along with a
benevolent heart, more than ordinary quickness and accuracy of

intellectual perception, may be left to the wise to determine" (67). Such a trait, combined with the ease with which Delano assumes and exercises his own authority, makes inevitable the type of appraisal he gives to the situation aboard the *San Dominick* and the conclusion that he draws from what he witnesses there.[7] Although Melville does not overtly refer to the inevitability of Captain Delano's conclusion, it is implied in Melville's remark that "to have beheld this undemonstrative invalid [Benito Cereno] gliding about, apathetic and mute, no landsman could have dreamed that in him was lodged a dictatorship beyond which, while at sea, there was no earthly appeal" (76). However incredible it might seem to the observer uninitiated in the ways of the sea, inexorable seafaring tradition forced Captain Delano to the conclusion that absolute authority resided in the person of Benito Cereno despite all evidence to the contrary.[8]

Until the moment in the narrative when Don Benito escapes from the *San Dominick*, the story has been told from the point of view of Amasa Delano. The authority of a ship captain has been examined in its various aspects based upon the assumption that this captain is actually in command of his ship. Once this mistaken notion is dispelled, the entire affair is described from a second point of view. The concluding portion of the tale is dealt with on the basis of the fact that the Negroes are in revolt, and many of the incidents that occurred prior to Don Benito's escape from his ship are re-examined.

In the lengthy extracts from the testimony of Benito Cereno, who gives his deposition during the trial of the mutineers, Melville clearly distinguishes between authority and power.[9] The drawing of this distinction is revealed in the many cruel and barbarous acts of the mutineers. During the time the Negroes were in command of the ship, power was exercised without authority. The mutineers, led by the wily Babo, have the power to act as they do after their successful revolt, but they have no authority, even though they have temporarily made ineffectual the authority of their captain. Don Benito's authority is based upon legal right; the Negroes' power is based upon force. Babo has led them in a reign of terror that tortured or killed progressively more Spaniards every time the Negroes' power was challenged. It is revealed that their final act of cruelty was the killing of the owner of the slaves and the nailing of his skeleton to the prow. They had led each white man to view the skeleton—and the motto they had inscribed beneath it, "Seguid vuestro jefe" (Follow your leader) —in an attempt to intimidate the Spaniards once and for all. Later when it became necessary for the mutineers to allow Captain Delano to board the ship, the use of the six hatchet-polishers to survey the scene was a naked display of power. Such devices are typical of the use of power without authority.

Although it is not possible to transfer authority by force, the authority of Don Benito and his officers was made ineffectual by their loss of power. The Spaniards were forced to submit to the rebelling slaves. Melville recognizes that once a captain's authority is overthrown it can only be replaced by the same agency that originally established it. Had the Americans arrived during the mutiny and aided in putting it down, the end of the narrative could have been different. Once the revolt was successful, only Spanish law could return the ship's government to order. In "Benito Cereno" the force represented by Captain Delano could only destroy the power of the mutineers. It became the task of the courts to restore authority.

The function of the law in relation to authority is demonstrated by Melville's conclusion to the tale. The law is an expression of the authority of the state. The law cannot command a ship, but the captain who does so derives his authority from maritime or naval law. When a captain's authority is destroyed, the law replaces it with that of another. Because of this traditional "chain of command," Melville's story involves mutiny without the death of the ship's captain. Benito Cereno's death would have removed him as a commander, but at the same time his authority would have passed to another of the Spanish officers. When he is held captive, dressed in the regalia of his office but stripped of his authority, Melville creates a situation in which the law is inoperative. The captain's loss of command is symbolized by the empty scabbard that he still wears:[10] "And that silver-mounted sword, apparent symbol of despotic command, was not, indeed, a sword, but the ghost of one. The scabbard, artificially stiffened, was empty" (169) . The power vacuum aboard the ship is temporarily filled, not by law but by the naked force employed by the mutineers to command obedience. When the power of the mutineers has in turn been overcome, the Spanish courts are in a position to restore legal power and authority to the *San Dominick* in the person of a new captain.

"Benito Cereno" is unique among Melville's tales and novels because it deals with a ship captain who has lost his command. This story alone illustrates certain aspects of Melville's general concept of the authority of the ship captain—a theme that appears in each of his novels dealing with the sea. Through his dual approach to the affair aboard the *San Dominick*, Melville demonstrates two things: first, the result of Don Benito's status as a ship captain without the power to enforce his commands; and, secondly, the misuse of power by usurping Negroes who rule without authority. The American captain, combining both authority and power, illustrates the ease with which command can be exercised under normal conditions. Chaos and disorder are the inevitable results of authority functioning without power and of power exercised without authority.

Whittier's Use of the *Sage*
in His Ballads

by
Harry Oster

IN MOST OF his poems based on folklore, John Greenleaf Whittier made use of the folk-tale type which folklorists call the *sage*. As Stith Thompson has described it, a *sage* "purports to be an account of an extraordinary happening believed to have actually occurred. It may recount a legend of something which happened in ancient times at a particular place . . . . It may tell of an encounter with marvelous creatures which the folk still believe in—fairies, ghosts, water-spirits, the Devil and the like. And it may give what has been handed down as a memory—often fantastic or absurd—of some historical character . . . . It will be observed that they are nearly always simple in structure, usually containing but a single narrative motif."[1]

One of Whittier's favorite sources for such material was Cotton Mather's history of New England, *Magnalia Christi Americana,* a work he read with particular care and interest. "The Garrison of Cape Ann" (1857) is a typical example of Whittier's artistic use of the "preternatural" events described in the *Magnalia.* The poem is based on an incident which occurred in 1692. In the words of Mather:

> there fell out a thing at Gloucester (on Cape Ann), which falls
> in here most properly to be related: A town so situated, sur-
> rounded and neiboured, in the county of Essex, that no man in
> his wits will imagine, that a dozen Frenchmen and Indians
> would come and alarm the inhabitants for three weeks togeth-

58

er, and engage 'em in several skirmishes while there were two regiments raised, a detachment of three-score men sent unto their succor and not one hurt in all the actions . . . . I entirely refer it unto thy judgment, (without the least offer of my own) whether Satan did not now "Set ambushments" against the good people of Gloucester, with daemons in the shape of armed Indians and Frenchmen, appearing to considerable numbers of the inhabitants, and mutually firing upon them for the best part of a month together. I know the most considerate gentlemen in the neighborhood unto this day believe the whole matter to have been a prodigious piece of the strange descent from the "invisible world," then made upon other parts of the country.[2]

Whittier expands this somewhat meager incident, giving it dramatic power and moral significance. In the garrison, as the soldiers are telling of strange supernatural events:

> Midnight came; from out the forest moved a dusky mass that soon
> Grew to warriors, plumed and painted, grimly marching in the moon.
> "Ghosts or witches," said the captain, "thus I foil the Evil One!"
> And he rammed a silver button from his doublet down his gun.[3]

The soldiers also fire at the spectre warriors, but their bullets are greeted with "a laugh of fierce derision." The captain, deciding that weapons are useless against the Devil's emissaries, leads his men in a prayer.

> Ceased thereat the mystic marching of the specters round the wall,
> But a sound abhorred, unearthly, smote the ears and hearts of all,
> Howls of rage and shrieks of anguish! Never after mortal man
> Saw the ghostly leaguers marching round the block-house of Cape Ann.

The poem concludes with this moral:

> Soon or late to all our dwellings come the spectres of
>   the mind,
> Doubts and fears and dread forbodings, in the darkness
>   undefined;
> Round us throng the grim projections of the heart and
>   of the brain,
> And our pride of strength is weakness, and the cunning
>   hand is vain.
> In the dark we cry like children; and no answer from
>   on high,
> Breaks the crystal spheres of silence, and no white wings
>   downward fly;
> But the heavenly help we pray for comes to faith, and not
>   to sight,
> And our prayers drive backward all the spirits of the
>   night.

Thus Whittier has treated a folk theme in typical fashion. The original account around which the poem is built is fragmentary; it is a *sage* with the single motif of spectre soldiers routed by prayer. The corresponding category in Stith Thompson's *Motif-Index of Folk Literature* is G303.16.2, "Devil's power over one avoided by prayer."[4] The poet has improved the story by giving it effective form and adding dramatic details. The routing of the spectres by prayer and the moral that faith alone can assure spiritual security are characteristic of his basic philosophy.[5]

Another poem which is somewhat indebted to the *Magnalia*, but to a lesser degree, is the early "The Spectre Ship" (1831). Whittier's introduction to the poem states:

> The legend of the Spectre Ship of Salem is still preserved among some of the old descendants of the puritans. A particular description of the preternatural visitation is given in *Magnalia Christi Americana*. The story is that a ship, which left Salem sometime during the 17th century for "old England", contained among other passengers, a young man of a strange and wild appearance, and a girl, still younger, and of surpassing beauty.

She was deadly pale, and trembled, even while she leaned on the arm of her companion. No one knew them—they spoke not— they paid no regard to anything around them. This excited the alarm of some of the credulous people of the place, who sup- posed them to be demons: and who is consequence, endeavored to dissuade their friends from entering the ship—notwithstand- ing which a goodly number went on board.[6]

The description of a spectre ship given in the *Magnalia* does not include any mention of the two strange passengers. When an American ship which had left the colonies in January, 1647, for England failed to return:

this put the godly people on much prayer, both publick and private, that the Lord would (if it was his pleasure) let them hear what he had done with their dear friends, and prepare them with a suitable submission to his Holy Will. In June next ensuing, a great thunderstorm arose out of the north-west after which (the hemisphere being serene) about an hour before sun- set, a SHIP of like dimensions with the aforesaid, with her can- vas and colours abroad (though the wind northernly) appeared in the air coming up from our harbour's mouth; which lyes southward from the town, seemingly with her sails filled under a fresh gale, holding her course north, and continuing under observation, sailing against the wind for the space of half an hour . . . . The admiring spectators could distinguish the sev- eral colours of each part, the principal rigging, and such pro- portion, as caused not only the generality of persons to say, "This was the mould of their ship, and thus was her tragick end," but Mr. Davenport also in publick declared to this effect, "That God had condescended, for the quieting of their afflicted spirits, this extraordinary account of his sovereign disposal of those for whom so many fervent prayers were made continual- ly."[7]

The demonic young couple must have come into the tale in the course of later oral tradition. In Mather's account as well as in Whittier's poem, the vessel, as do most ghost ships, sails against the wind, a motif classified as F411.3 in the *Motif-Index*, "Demon ship sails against the wind," and the revelation of the fate of the ship and passengers falls into the category of E535.3, "sight of a phantom ship a bad omen." However, the moral significance attached to the tradition by the Puritans was not included by Whittier; evidently in his youth he was not addicted to tacking moral endings onto ballads.

> Near and more near the ship came on,
>   With all her broad sails spread—
> The night grew thick, but a phantom light
>   Around her deck was shed
> And the gazers shuddered as on she came,
>   For against the wind she sped.
>
> They saw by the dim and baleful glare
>   Around that voyager thrown,
> The upright forms of the well-known crew,
>   As pale and fixed as stone—
> And they called to them, but no sound came back,
>   Save the echoed cry alone.
>
> The fearful stranger-youth was there,
>   And clasped in his embrace,
> The pale and passing sorrowful
>   Gazed wildly in his face;
> Like one who had been wakened from
> The silent burial-place.
> . . . .
> And lo! the vision passed away—
>   The Spectre Ship—the crew—
> The stranger and his pallid bride,
>   Departed from their view;
> And nought was left upon the waves
>   Beneath the arching blue.
>
> It passed away—that vision strange—
>   Forever from their sight,—
> Yet, long shall Naumkeag's annals tell
>   The story of that night,—
> The phantom-bark—the ghostly crew—
>   The pale, encircling light.[8]

Whittier also wrote ballads on the subject of witchcraft, based on the many New England stories in print and in oral circulation. His imagination was stirred particularly by the traditions about Eunice (Goody) Cole, a resident of Hampton, New Hampshire, in the latter half of the seventeenth century. When she was indicted for witchcraft in 1673, the court decided: "In ye case of Unis Cole now prisoner att ye Bar not legally guilty according to Inditement butt just ground of vehement suspissyon of her haveing had famillyarryty with the devill."[9]

Whittier was so struck by the colorfulness of the stories being told about her that he included her as a central figure in two of his poems, "The Wreck of the Rivermouth" (1846) and "The Changeling" (1865). In his introduction to the former, Whittier writes: "The Goody Cole who figures in this poem and *The Changeling* was Eunice Cole, who for a quarter of a century or more was feared, persecuted, and hated as the witch of Hampton. She lived alone in a hovel a little distant from the spot where the Hampton Academy now stands, and there she died unattended. When her death was discovered, she was hastily covered up in the earth near by, and a stake driven through her body to exorcise the evil spirit."[10]

The poem tells how a girl on a ship sailing down the Hampton River to the sea jeers at Goody Cole with dire results:

> "Fie on the witch!" cried a merry girl,
>   As they round the point where Goody Cole
> Sat by her door with her wheel atwirl,
>   A bent and blear-eyed poor old soul.
> "Oho!" she muttered, "Ye're brave to-day!
>   But I hear the little waves laugh and say
> 'The broth will be cold that waits at home;
>   For it's one to go, but another to come.'"

The ship goes down in a storm at sea:

> Goody Cole looked out from her door:
>   The Isles of Shoals were drowned and gone.
> Scarcely she saw the Head of the Boar
>   Toss the foam from tusks of stone.

> She clasped her hands with grip of pain,
>   The tear on her cheek was not of rain:
> "They are lost," she muttered, "boat and crew!
> Lord, forgive me! my words were true!"

At the funeral, only the old ex-minister of the town, Father
Bachiler, who is in disgrace for having married a woman of "doubtful fame," shows any sympathy for her while:

> Old Goody Cole looked drearily round
>   As two by two, with their faces hid,
> The mourners walked to the burying ground.
>   She let the staff from her clasped hands fall:
> "Lord, forgive us! We're sinners all!"[11]

Actually since the records show that Goody Cole had been
thrown into prison in 1656, where she still was at the time of the
wreck in 1657, and "Father Bachiler" had gone to England in
1654 or 1655,[12] the events in the poem could not have occurred.
Whittier probably took the first motif in his poem, mockery of
witch leads to disaster (roughly Q288 in the *Motif-Index*, "punishment for mockery"), from a local tradition; however, the second
motif, the repentance of the supposed witch at the fulfillment of
her prophecy, and the third motif, her praying for forgiveness at
the funeral, are not typical folk motifs. It seems likely that Whittier added them himself to round out the story and to express
his sympathy for the persecuted.

"The Changeling" (1865), a much better poem in its ability to
arouse a mood of supernatural dread, tells the weird tale of Anna
Favor, who had a mad, obsessive belief that her own baby had
been stolen away by Goody Cole and replaced with a witch child.
Insanely the wife demands:

> "Rake out the red coals, goodman,—
>   For there the child shall lie,
> Till the black witch comes to fetch her
>   And both up the chimney fly."

Her husband prays God to

> "Let her sight come back, and clothe her
>   Once more in her right mind,"

and the cloud is lifted from her soul. Then, she dispatches her husband to save Goody Cole. The final verses have the music and movement of an ancient folk ballad:

> His horse he saddled and bridled.
>   And into the night rode he,
> Now through the great black woodland,
>   Now by the white-beached sea.
>
> He rode through the silent clearings,
>   He came to the ferry wide,
> And thrice he called to the boatman
>   Asleep on the other side.
>
> He set his horse to the river,
>   He swam to Newbury town,
> And he called up Justice Sewall
>   In his nightcap and his gown.
> . . . .
> Then through the night the hoof-beats
>   Went sounding like a flail;
> And Goody Cole at cockcrow
>   Came forth from Ipswich jail.[13]

The folk motif around which the poem is built comes closest to P231.6, "mother casts out dull, stupid changeling."

Perhaps Whittier's best poem on the subject of witchcraft is "The Witch of Wenham." The *sage* (the central motif is not included in the *Motif-Index*) from which the story is taken is told by the poet in the introduction to the poem: "The house is still standing in Danvers, Massachusetts, where, it is said, a suspected witch was confined overnight in the attic, which was bolted fast. In the morning when the constable came to take her to Salem for trial, she was missing, although the door was still bolted. Her

escape . . . at the time was attributed to Satanic interference."[14]
Out of this slight material Whittier wove a fine tale. A daring
youth is in love with a beautiful girl who is believed to be be-
witched. His mother pleads:

> "Son Andrew, for the love of God,
>   And of thy mother stay!"
> She clasped her hands, she wept aloud,
>   But Andrew rode away.

Meanwhile the girl is put in prison to await punishment, and
her protestations of innocence are ignored.

> "Oh, leave me for my mother's sake,
>   She needs my eyes to see."
> "Those eyes, young witch, the crows shall peck
>   From off the gallows-tree."

While she was in prison:

> Oh weird and still the dark hours passed;
>   No human sound she heard
> But up and down the chimneystack
>   The swallows moaned and stirred.
>
> And o'er her with a dread surmise,
>   Of evil sight and sound,
> The blind bats on their leathern wings
>   Went wheeling round and round.
>
> Low hanging in the midnight sky,
>   Looked in a half-faced moon,
> Was it a dream, or did she hear
>   Her lover's whistled tune?

Defying parental, civil, and religious law, the lover steals her
out of prison:

> He set her on his pillion soft,
>   Her arms about him twined;

> And noiseless as if velvet-shod
> They left the house behind.[15]

In this poem, Whittier has taken a short fragment of folklore and transformed it into a poem which contains much of the form, mood, movement, and music of traditional balladry. Fortunately, this time Whittier states no moral, but merely broadens the story to include the shaking off by New England of the haunting horror of witchcraft.[16]

Whittier was fascinated not only by the stories of Puritan days, but also by those circulating in his day, dealing with events of the recent past.

About "The New Wife and the Old," a ballad written in 1843, Whittier tells us, in an introductory note, that it is "founded upon one of the marvelous legends, connected with the famous General M. of Hampton, New Hampshire, who was regarded by his neighbors as a Yankee Faust, in league with the adversary."[17]

M., about whom the legend was told, was a real person, General Jonathan Moulton, who had fought the Abenaki Warriors.

Another part of the legend about Moulton deals with his marriage to a young woman, after his first wife had died under suspicious circumstances. In the middle of the night, the bride feels the ghostly hand of the first Mrs. Moulton taking off the wedding ring. When the candles are lighted and search has been made, it becomes clear that the ghost has taken away the jewelry which was once hers.[18]

It is this motif—E221, "dead spouse's malevolent return," or perhaps E222.1, "dead wife haunts husband on second marriage"—which is taken by Whittier as the central incident in his ballad, "The New Wife and the Old." The scene opens on the wedding night; as the young girl and her middle-aged husband lie together in bed:

> From the brief dream of a bridge
> She hath wakened at his side.
> With half-uttered shriek and start—
> Feels she not his beating heart?
> And the pressure of his arm,
> And his breathing near and warm?[19]

As she is reassuring herself of her husband's love, and admiring again the costly jewels he has given her, suddenly:

> Ha!—that start of horror! why
> That wild stare and wilder cry,
> Full of terror, full of pain?
> Is there madness in her brain?
> Hark! that grasping, hoarse and low,
> "Spare me,—spare me,—let me go!"
>
> God have mercy!—icy cold
> Spectral hands her own enfold,
> Drawing from them
> Love's fair gifts of gold and gem,
> "Waken! save me!" still as death
> At her side he slumbereth.

He wakes up, and his disbelief of the spectral visit is shattered by the absence of the jewels.

> Broken words of cheer he saith,
> But his dark lip quivereth,
> And as o'er the past he thinketh,
> From his wife's young arm he shrinketh;
> Can those soft arms round him lie,
> Underneath his dead wife's eye?

The final moral is:

> And the tenderest and the weakest
> Who their wrongs have borne the meekest,
> Lifting from those dark, still places,
> Sweet and sad-remembered faces,
> O'er the guilty hearts behind
> An unwitting triumph find.

On the whole, the story is well told, though there is a good deal of triteness. Also, though the poem is only twenty-one stanzas long, there are three stanzas of moral at the end, where one would have served the purpose more effectively.

As was true of his use of Colonial *sage*, Whittier's interest in folklore as material for poetry was not limited to what he learned directly from the oral tradition. The excellent poem, "The Dead Ship of Harpswell" (1866), is a case in support of this very point.

The ghost-ship story grew up around an actual vessel, the *Dash*, which plunged among the breakers off Georges Bank in 1815. No trace of the ship or its crew was ever found.[20]

How the story got to Whittier is told in a letter written to a freind in 1889: "Some twenty-five years ago, I received from Miss Marion Pearl, daughter of the Reverend Mr. Pearl, a well-known clergyman of Maine, a letter descriptive of the people, dialects, customs, superstitions, and legends of Orris Island, where I think the writer was a teacher. The legend of a spectre ship as described in my poem, attracted me by its weird suggestiveness."[21]

It was said that after the wreck of the *Dash*, the fisherfolk of Maine often saw the form of a ship, with gaunt timbers showing through the planks, float shoreward toward the harbor at Harpswell. Whether in calm or storm, income or outgo of tide, the ghost ship continued until it nearly reached the shore, and then, as she neared the rocks, the ship would pause, then float away, rudder foremost, vanishing in the twilight. After its appearance, burial boats, when they crossed the harbor, were somehow forced by wind, tide, or current to follow the course previously taken by the ghost ship.[22] These motifs fit roughly into the same categories as those in "The Spectre ship," E411.3, "demon ship sails against the wind," and E535.3, "sight of a phantom ship a bad omen."

Whittier has taken this *sage* and made it into a ballad which at times effectively evokes a mood of supernatural dread. The best lines are the following:

> What weary doom of baffled quest,
> Thou sad sea ghost is thine?
> What makes thee in the haunts of home
> A wonder and a sign?
>
> . . . .
>
> Shake brown old wives, with dreary joy,
> Your gray-head hints of ill;
> And, over sick-beds whispering low,
> Your prophecies fulfill.

> Some home amid yon birchen trees
> Shall drape its door with woe;
> And slowly where the Dead Ship sails,
> The burial boat shall row![23]

This picture of the old women direly and yet gleefully predicting death in the wake of the spectre ship is spine-chilling in its impact. However, the moral—that the approach of death is not to be feared since it comes at the will of God—is stated too directly for modern tastes in poetry.

One of the best examples of Whittier's skill as a writer of ballads is his masterful *Skipper Ireson's Ride*. Though the poem is based on an actual incident, the story reached Whittier through oral channels, and, like a folk tale, developed and changed in the course of transmission. The incident of Benjamin Ireson, who was nicknamed "Flood," occurred in 1808. Though he did not complete the poem until 1857, Whittier first heard a tale about Ireson and the rhyme out of which he made his refrain, in 1828 from a schoolmate, a native of Marblehead. The variant Whittier heard from him was probably much like the one quoted in the *Boston Evening Transcript* of June 12, 1837, described as being composed and sung by the boys of Marblehead.

> Old Flood Ireson for his hord hort
> Was torred and feathered and carried in a cart.
> Old Flood Ireson for leaving the wreck
> Was torred and feathered all up to his neck.
> Old Flood Ireson for his great sin
> Was torred and feathered all up to his chin.
> Old Flood Ireson for his bad behavior
> Was torred and feathered and carried to Salem.[24]

A valuable insight into the story which was circulating orally is found in the recollections of a British actor, Tyrone Power, who was touring America some twenty-five years later. In his *Impressions of America, During the Years 1833, 1834, and 1835*, Power wrote on the subject of Marblehead:

The population is famous for its industry and for the summary mode with which they dispense justice amongst themselves on local polity affecting the general weal. One instance was a townsman, returning from the Banks with a cargo, passed a vessel in a sinking state, turning a blind eye to their repeated anxious signals. Contrary to all expectations, the crippled bark, after being given up as lost, reached the harbour, and the conduct of the hard-hearted skipper was made public. He was seized *instanter*, triced up, covered with tar, clothed in feathers, and in this plight carted about the boundaries of the township, having a label hung about his neck that described his crime and sentence with good set rhymes, which ran as follows:

> This here's old John Hort
> That for his hard heart,
> Is tar-ed and feather-ed
> And carry-ed in this cart.[25]

This version was also circulating in Marblehead:

> Old Flood Oirson for his hord hort
> Was tor'd and further'd and coried in a cort,
> A becos he left five men on a wrack,
> Was tor'd and further'd all over his back.[26]

An allegedly historical account of the incident of the unfortunate skipper appeared in 1880, in the *History and Traditions of Marblehead* by Samuel Roads, in which the author maintained that the crew, not Captain Ireson, was responsible for leaving the sinking ship, and that they lied on returning to port in order to protect themselves. Also, the account by Roads stated that the Captain had been tarred and feathered, and carried on his disgraceful ride by the men and boys of the town, not the women of Marblehead, as in Whittier's ballad refrain.[27]

Whittier read the account by Roads, and accepted his version as the true one; in a letter which he instructed should be published with the poem in subsequent editions of his works, he gracefully acknowledged himself mistaken in the facts of the case. The story on which his ballad was based was apparently not very detailed, for in the letter Whittier wrote: "I supposed the story to which it referred dated back at least a century. I knew nothing of the participators, and the narrative of the ballad was pure fancy."[28]

Whatever the true facts may have been, whether the Skipper or the crew was guilty (a matter of whose word one accepts), one does arrive at significant insights into how the artistry of Whittier transformed a simple *sage* into an excellent ballad. It is obvious that Whittier took little pains with checking the facts of the tale; he preferred to tell it along the lines suggested by his schoolmate from Marblehead, probably because in its oral form it had already acquired the quality of folklore. (The central motif is not in the *Motif-Index.*)

Since the three versions quoted above of the rhymes chanted by the villagers, and the account of Power, fail to mention the women of Marblehead, and since Whittier himself said "The narrative of the ballad was pure invention," we may conclude that their role in the poem was invented by Whittier, or at least greatly expanded. Whittier's picture of

> Old Floyd Ireson, for his hard heart,
> Tarred and feathered and carried in a cart,
>   By the women of Marblehead,

makes the narrative much more powerful than it would have been had the unfortunate skipper been pushed around by men. In a highly effective manner Whittier has depicted the normally gentle village women acting as savagely as those of the French Revolution cheering on the sweep of the guillotine:

> Wrinkled scolds with hands on hips,
> Girls in bloom of cheek and lips,
> Wild-eyed, free-limbed, such as chase
> Bacchus round some antique vase,
> Brief of skirt, with ankles bare,
> With conch-shells blowing and fish-horns' twang,
> Over and over the Maenads sang,
>   "Here's Flud Oirson, fur his horrd horrt,

> Torr'd and furtherr'd an' corr'd in a corrt
> By the women of Morblehead."

This refrain owes much of its effect to the fact that it is in the local dialect. The dialect was not Whittier's idea, but a suggestion of James Russell Lowell, then the editor of the *Atlantic Monthly*, in which the poem made its first appearance in 1857. This refrain is the only instance in Whittier's poetry of the use of a local New England dialect. Perhaps, like Frost, he believed that a dialect has to be heard to be communicated.

Finally, the poem is brought to a satisfactory conclusion in a manner expressive of Whittier's strong moral sense. The village women believe his cry that the "nameless horror that lives within" is a far greater shame to him than the ride in the cart. Their savagery gives way to Christian feeling:

> Then the wife of the skipper lost at sea
> Said, "God has touched him, why should we?"
> Said an old wife mourning her only son,
> "Cut the rogue's tether and let him run!"
> So with soft relentings and rude excuse,
> Half scorn, half pity, they cut him loose,
> And gave him a cloak to hide him in,
> And left him alone with his shame and sin,
>   Poor Floyd Ireson, for his hard heart,
>   Tarred and feathered and carried in a cart
>   By the women of Marblehead.[29]

The stirring ballad "Barbara Frietchie" contains elements of folklore, though Whittier himself did not realize it when he wrote the poem. One of the few on-the-spot accounts of Stonewall Jackson's march through Frederick town, which was written by a Union army surgeon stationed there, states: "Jackson, I did not get a look at to recognize him, though I must have seen him, as I witnessed the passage of all the troops through the town."[30] The surgeon makes no mention of any incident involving Barbara Frietchie. He would probably have mentioned it if it had occurred.

Also, Dr. Oliver Wendell Holmes, shortly after the appearance of Stonewall Jackson in Frederick, passed through the town on his trip to find his son, who had been badly wounded at Antietam. Dr. Holmes, it seems likely, would have heard about the incident, if it had taken place, and included it among the war reminiscences of *My Hunt for the Captain.*

Additional evidence is of a much more tangible nature. There was a real Barbara Frietchie in Frederick, over "fourscore and ten," and she did have a flag, but from that point what actually occurred diverges from the story heard by Whittier. The niece and adopted daughter of Barbara Frietchie, a Mrs. Handschue, inherited the flag. The flag, which still belongs to the family, is torn, but not "rent . . . with seam and gash," from a "rifle blast," as Whittier declares in the poem. Mrs. Handschue has stated that Barbara Frietchie never waved the flag at Jackson's men.[31] According to Barbara Frietchie's relatives, she waved her flag at the Northern troops, under Burnside, who marched through the town six days after Jackson. Mrs. Handschue's daughter, Mrs. Abbott, wrote of the incident thus:

Jackson and his men had been in Frederick and had left a short time before. We were glad that the rebels had gone and that our troops came. My mother and I lived almost opposite aunt's place. She and my mother's cousin, Harriet Yoner, lived together. Mother said I should go and see aunt and tell her not to be frightened. You know that aunt was then almost ninety-six years old. When I reached aunt's place she knew as much as I did about matters, and cousin Harriet was with her. They were on the front porch, and aunt was leaning on the cane she always carried. When the troops marched along aunt waved her hand, and cheer after cheer went up from the men as they saw her. Some even ran into the yard. "God bless you, dear old soul," cried one after the other, as they rushed into the yard. Aunt being rather feeble, and in order to save her as much as we could, cousin Harriet Yoner said, "Aunt ought to have a flag to wave." The flag was hidden in the family Bible, and cousin Harriet got it and gave it to aunt. Then she waved the flag to the men and they cheered her as they went by. She was very patriotic and the troops all knew of her. The day before General

Reno was killed he came to see aunt and had a talk with her.[32]

From the raw material of these facts grew a pretty *sage* of heroic defiance, the development of which can still be traced. Some time after the invasion of 1862, a lady from Frederick paid a visit to Washington. There she told her friends the story of the courage of old Barbara Frietchie. As usually happens when a story passes from mouth to mouth, significant changes occurred in the tale. Finally Mrs. E. D. E. N. Southworth, a novelist living in Washington, wrote Whittier a letter telling him about Barbara Frietchie and describing as fact the legend that had by now grown up of the incident between Stonewall Jackson and the stalwart old lady. Mrs. Southworth wrote as follows:

> When on the morning of the 6th of September, the advance of Lee's army, led by the formidable rebel general "Stonewall" Jackson, entered Frederick, every Union flag was lowered, and the halliards cut; every store and every dwelling-house was closed; the inhabitants had retreated indoors; the streets were deserted, and, to quote the official report, "the city wore a churchyard aspect." But Mrs. Barbara Frietchie, taking one of the Union flags, went up to the top of her house, opened a garret window, and held it forth. The rebel army marched up the street, saw the flag; the order was given, "Halt! Fire!" and a volley was discharged at the window from which it was displayed. The flag-staff was partly broken, so that the flag drooped; the old lady drew it in, broke off the fragment, and, taking the stump with the flag still attached to it in her hand, stretched herself as far out the window as she could, held the stars and the stripes at arm's length, waving over the rebels, and cried out in a voice of indignation and sorrow: "Fire at this old head, then, boys: it is not more venerable than your flag." They fired no more; they passed in silence and with downcast looks; and she secured the flag in its place, where it waved unmolested during the whole of the rebel occupation of the city. "Stonewall" would not permit her to be troubled. The rebel army evacuated Frederick on the 11th, and our troops, under General Burnside, entered on the 12th.[33]

Whittier was sure it was a true story, and tried to follow the details given him as closely as possible in the poem he published in

1863 in the *Atlantic Monthly*. When the authenticity of the story was first questioned, Whittier remarked: "That there was a Dame Frietchie in Frederick who loved the old flag is not disputed by any one. As for the rest I do not feel responsible. If there was no such occurrence, so much the worse for Frederick City."[34]

After a while, Whittier began to get peevish at the many attacks which had been made on the validity of the story; he wrote a letter to the *Century* magazine defending himself: "The poem 'Barbara Frietchie' was written in good faith. The story was no invention of mine. It came to me from sources which I regarded as entirely reliable; it had been published in newspapers, and had gained public credence in Washington and Maryland before my poem was written. I had no reason to doubt its accuracy then, and I am still constrained to believe that it had a foundation in fact. If I thought otherwise, I should not hesitate to express it. I have no pride of authorship to interfere with my allegiance to truth."[35]

However, eventually he recovered his usual good humor, and in 1890, a couple of years before his death, he wrote a much more urbane and less positive statement to one of the many friends who had asked him whether the story was a myth: "I had a portrait of the good Lady Barbara from the saintly hand of Dorothea Dix, whose life is spent in works of love and duty, and a cane from Barbara's cottage, sent me by Dr. Steiner of the Maryland Senate. Whether she did all that my poem ascribed to her or not, she was a brave and true woman. I followed the account given me in a private letter and in the papers of the time."[36]

In effect, then, Whittier took as his raw material a single motif *sage* from written sources. (The motif is not included in the *Motif-Index*.) Out of this material Whittier fashioned a stirring ballad, although unfortunately the poem has traces of the sentimentality and overmoralizing which often mar his poems. For example, having "a blush of shame" suffuse the face of Stonewall Jackson hardly suits the stern, dedicated general.

To conclude, it was Whittier's frequent practice to hunt up a picturesque motif, a *sage*, to expand and dramatize the incident until it became a well-rounded account, and to conclude the poem in keeping wih his Christian philosophy. Usually, he was primarily interested in the folk version of an incident, and seldom bothered to check his historical facts with precision; he found the folk account of an event the proper raw material for his ends of entertainment and instruction.

Tragic Consciousness in Isabel Archer

by

John Roland Dove

I

As HENRY JAMES tells us in his Preface, *The Portrait of a Lady* is concerned with "a certain young woman affronting her destiny." Her destiny turns on betrayal like that of so many other characters in James's novels. She discovers that the man whom she had considered "the most civilized man in the world" is a shallow egotist who had married her for her money. Her marriage proves an impasse that is devoid of love, understanding, and true reciprocity.

As though to call attention to the banality inhering in something so commonplace as a marital disillusion, James provides Isabel with relatives who are, like herself, disappointed in marriage. The impact of such a disillusion varies, however, from person to person, and Isabel has none of the philosophical resignation of her uncle, Mr. Touchett, and none of the shrill-mouthed insouciance of her sister-in-law, the Countess Gemini, to sustain her during her time of sorrow. Her discovery of Osmond's true nature and her subsequent recognition of the failure of her marriage is, indeed, an emotional and spiritual shock of such grave personal import that it modifies her whole attitude toward life.

The extent of Isabel's disillusion can only be understood in terms of her character. Isabel's character has, however, been subject to much critical misrepresentation. Rebecca West, for example, considers her "far too radiantly good for this world"; Oscar Cargill thinks she is sexually inhibited; Quentin Anderson thinks she is "ignorant, self-centered, and afraid."[1] None of these interpretations does justice to Isabel or provides any adequate explanation of the rationale behind her marriage to Gilbert Osmond. Critics have failed to recognize that in addition to being one of James's most individualized characters, Isabel Archer also belongs to a very sharply defined type. As I shall demonstrate, she is a thorough-going romantic with the true romantic's longing for self-surrender and self-education. She is an idealist and a perfectionist whose basic problem is to find a *modus vivendi* that will be both morally and emotionally satisfying. She sees in Gilbert Osmond a heaven-sent answer to her problem. She erroneously considers him good, just, and noble, and in dedicating herself to him she dedicates herself to everything she believes he represents. She assumes that they will be able to achieve an ideally reciprocal relationship, and she believes that such a relationship with such a man will completely satisfy her hunger for perfection.

Isabel Archer is, as James makes clear, fundamentally irrational like all idealists, and in marrying Gilbert Osmond she is guilty of "great folly." She is always willing to defy common sense in the interest of her dreams and insists on idealizing Osmond in the teeth of all the evidence and in obstinate disregard of the warnings she receives from her aunt and from her cousin. James, however, never approaches Isabel in the spirit of what he calls "scientific criticism." He sympathizes with her rather than ridicules her, and sets himself the task of showing that her folly is the outcome of a temperament both generous and trusting. She overestimates Osmond because she naively assumes that the man of sensibility and taste is *ex hypothesi* a virtuous man. Granted her Albany background and her inexperience of Europe, such an error could not be more natural. She is a victim of what I shall call "the myth of civility"—the mythical idea, that is to say, that a necessary correlation exists between the virtues that characterize the "civilized man," such as intelligence, tact, sensibility, and urbanity, and the virtues that characterize the man of conscience, such as integrity, goodness of heart, and unselfishness. Married life with Osmond opens her eyes to the bitterly paradoxical truth that it is possible to be at once completely civilized and completely selfish.

Isabel Archer is the victim of another myth, which I shall call "the romantic myth of reciprocity." She enters marriage with an idealized conception of the possibilities inherent in a personal relationship. She expects more from Osmond than the usual companionship of married life. She expects a companionship of the spirit. She believes that Osmond will satisfy all the desires of her heart and her soul; she commits herself to him completely as one might commit oneself to a church or a political cause. Her appeal for reciprocity is, however, denied. Osmond rejects all her demands for affection and understanding. The result is that for the first time in her life Isabel becomes conscious of her own isolation as a human being. She is flung back on herself, and she realizes that it is with herself that she must always live. She surrenders all belief in the redemptive powers of a personal relationship. Married life, ironically, teaches Isabel to come to terms with her basic solitude.

Isabel's disillusion with Osmond is, then, a disillusion with the ideals that he had represented to her. Bitter experience teaches her that these ideals were mythical constructs bearing no relation to reality. Her disillusion is at the same time an enlightenment. In James's hands, however, it is essentially a tragic enlightenment. He has sufficient sympathy with her idealism, naive as it is, to deplore its refutation. His own romanticism causes him to identify himself with the romanticism of his heroine. As a man who was himself equally sensitive to the claims of a simple morality and to the claims of that highly sophisticated civilization which it is so convenient to classify under the heading of "Europe," James was in a position to do justice to Isabel's equation of morality and civility. Such an equation, Isabel discovers, does not hold true in the world as it is, but she feels—and it is clear that James feels the same way—that it should hold true and that it is nothing short of a tragic fact that it does not. James also does justice to the romantic myth of reciprocity that causes Isabel to expect so much. He relates this myth to the inner necessities of her temperament. She needs desperately, like all romantics, to dedicate herself completely and to be accepted completely. The ingenuous belief that Osmond will meet these demands is after its fashion a signal act of good faith, however misplaced. Its betrayal is a personal catastrophe. She gazes into a future of unredeemed solitude and realizes that the deepest demands of her nature will forever be denied.

Isabel Archer may be described as a person whose real "destiny" is to eat of the fruit of "The Tree of Knowledge "and to find it bitter. She acquires through her disillusion a new consciousness of life which may be called a tragic consciousness. She sees in Osmond a terrible instance of the dichotomy between sensibility and conscience; she sees in herself the dilemma of human loneliness.

II

The young woman whom Mrs. Touchett discovers sitting by herself in the "office" of her Albany home, attempting to come to terms with a history of German thought, impresses her aunt as an independent girl fond of her own way. She seems a self-contained and self-assured young woman who treasures her freedom of thought and action above everything. She exhibits, indeed, an avowed distaste for dependence on anyone, even a close relative. At Gardencourt, she is quick to refute Ralph's imputation that she has been "adopted" by Mrs. Touchett. "Oh, no," she exclaims firmly, "she has not adopted me. I'm not a candidate for adoption." She is ready to listen to any advice her aunt has to give her on questions involving European manners, but she insists from the first on the prerogative of making her own decisions.

Isabel's attitude to Mrs. Touchett is characteristic of the girl who in the name of her independence rejects both Caspar Goodwood and Lord Warburton. Critics have failed to notice, however, that there is a certain speciousness about Isabel's cult of independence. She is not as confident in herself as she appears to be. In complete contrast to Henrietta Stackpole, that aggressive incarnation of American self-reliance, Isabel is subject to innumerable doubts and misgivings. She is, for example, unable to justify her dismissal of her suitors to herself with complete success. Her inheritance, moreover, raises more problems than it solves. The freedom that it brings confronts her with perplexing dilemmas of moral responsibility. "A large fortune means freedom," she confesses to Ralph, "and I'm afraid of that . . . . I'm not sure that it's not a greater happiness to be powerless" (I, 320) .[2]

Isabel is a prey to misgivings because of her innate perfectionism. She measures her conduct against the most exacting standards and, naturally enough, finds it wanting. "She was always planning out her development, desiring her perfection, observing her progress," James tells us. To desire to live the perfect life is, nevertheless, a far cry from knowing how to live it. Isabel longs to be above reproach, but her moral ideals tend to be inflated and confused. "Her thoughts," writes James in a long passage of analysis, "were a tangle of vague outlines which had never been corrected by the judgment of people speaking with authority." She has, however, "an unquenchable desire to think well of herself," and "she spent half of her time in thinking of beauty and bravery and magnanimity." She even hopes to "find herself in a difficult position, so that she should have the pleasure of being as heroic as the occasion demanded" (I, 67-69) . She is, in a word, an idealistic young woman whose passionate faith in the future presupposes that the future will in some way or other provide the directive she needs. Her appetite for life is an appetite for the perfect life. She is a restless and questing spirit who yearns to commit herself to some cause in which she may completely believe. She treasures her independence because, paradoxically, she is searching for some satisfactory way of losing it.

Before meeting Osmond, Isabel is inclined to dismiss out of hand the possibility that she might be able to realize her ideals by means of marriage. She associates her "free exploration of life" with a vague campaign of self-improvement, and the "beauty and bravery and magnanimity" of which she dreams seem to have reference to herself alone. James suggests to us, however, that Isabel's indifference to matters of the heart is assumed rather than real. "Deep in her soul—it was the deepest thing there—lay a belief that if a certain light should dawn she could give herself completely; but this image, on the whole, was too formidable to be attractive" (I, 71-72) . In other words, she is a woman who pretends to herself that she is superior to romantic emotions because she is only too well aware of the strength and power of these emotions. When Gilbert Osmond proposes to her, she is frightened.

"What made her dread great," writes James, "was precisely the force which, as it would seem, ought to have banished all dread—the sense of something within herself, deep down, that she supposed to be inspired and trustful passion. It was there like a large sum stored in a bank—which there was a terror in having to begin to spend. If she touched it, it would all come out" (II, 18).

Critics like Oscar Cargill explain Isabel's dread of self-surrender in terms of a characteristically Puritan dread of sex.[3] Isabel, they say, is the sexually inhibited daughter of a Puritan culture. According to this view, Isabel rejects Caspar Goodwood and Lord Warburton because she is made nervous by their aggressive masculinity, while she accepts Gilbert Osmond because he is so detached, so unimpassioned, and, comparatively speaking, so sexless. This point of view seems to me fallacious. Isabel's dread of self-surrender is the reverse side of a longing for self-surrender that she refuses to indulge until she meets someone worthy of such surrender. Until such a person appears, she prefers to dismiss romantic considerations from her mind. Because a sexual dedication is a dedication of her whole being, she has to be morally enticed before she will commit herself sexually, and, naturally enough, she is alarmed at the prospect of marriage since marriage involves for her absolute and unconditional surrender. The passage quoted above shows clearly that Isabel recognizes that in marrying Osmond she will be called upon to spend to the last penny the large sum of passion stored, as James's metaphor has it, in the bank. This is surely not the attitude of a repressed and inhibited young Puritan!

Why does Isabel reject Caspar Goodwood and Lord Warburton, both of them, as it turns out, much more worthy of her love than Gilbert Osmond? She tries to persuade herself that she rejects them in the cause of her independence. "She couldn't marry Lord Warburton; the idea failed to support any enlightened prejudice in favour of the free life that she had hitherto entertained or was now capable of entertaining" (I, 155). It is obvious, nevertheless, that Isabel is not really convinced by her own arguments. There is a rationale underlying her attitude to her suitors that escapes her. She is puzzled at her own bravado in discouraging candidates for her hand whom in so many ways she admires and respects.

"Who was she, what was she, that she should hold herself superior?" she asks herself after Lord Warburton's proposal. She is perplexed at her own fastidiousness, though it is entirely in accordance with her character. She is not in love with Caspar Goodwood or Lord Warburton because neither of them appeals to her moral imagination. Lord Warburton offers her a glamorous social position, while Caspar Goodwood offers her his own brand of masculine ardor, but both of them offer her little more than the routine duties of married life. Isabel longs for higher duties and more glowing responsibilities. Worthy as they are, neither of them appears to her worthy of her ultimate surrender. Although she does not acknowledge it, she is in true romantic fashion waiting for one who will reflect as in a mirror all her ideals. She tells Ralph equivocally that she rejected Lord Warburton because he was "too good" for her. His reply is extremely perspicacious. "As a fact," he says, "you think nothing in the world too good for you."

Isabel's great need is to clarify her ideals to herself and to focus them, and in the light of this necessity her encounter with Madame Merle is of inestimable importance. This woman, the most gracious and the most civilized that Isabel has ever met, is to affect the whole course of Isabel's life by promoting her marriage with Osmond, but her influence reaches far beyond sinister stratagems. She opens up new vistas for Isabel. She inspires her with a new ideal—the ideal of the life of civility. In a way that she does not realize, Madame Merle is from the first the subtle advocate of Osmond. The qualities that Isabel prizes so much in Osmond—his urbanity, his sensibility, his sense of form—are the qualities that Madame Merle, his mistress, has taught her how to appreciate.

Isabel, who longs to know how to live, sees in Madame Merle a woman who has mastered the secret of life. "Our heroine," writes James, "had always passed for a person of resources and had taken a certain pride in being one; but she wandered, as by the wrong side of the wall of a private garden, round the enclosed talents, accomplishments, aptitudes, of Madame Merle. She found herself desiring to emulate them, and in twenty such ways this lady presented herself as a model. 'I should like awfully to be *so!*' Isabel exclaimed more than once as one after another of her friend's fine aspects caught the light, and before long she knew that she had learned a lesson from a high authority" (I, 270). At times, it is true, Madame Merle's mask drops sufficiently for Isabel to catch a passing glimpse of the crass worldliness of her motives, but until she is presented with the most irrefutable evidence to the contrary, she insists on regarding Madame Merle as a "great lady" and a "good influence." For Isabel, Madame Merle is a great artist— an artist in living. She is, unhappily, completely unaware that there is no necessary correlation between goodness and a good impression. The fact that Madame Merle is pre-eminently pleas- ing is proof enough to Isabel that she is pre-eminently good.

If Madame Merle is the most exceptional woman whom Isabel has met, Gilbert Osmond is the most exceptional man. Isabel finds in Osmond the qualities she had admired in Madame Merle en- hanced by a subtle masculine appeal. As he shows her his treasures in his Florentine villa, she feels that "she had never met a person of so fine a grain." She is impressed by his exquisite sensibility, and not without reason. He is intelligent and in many ways per- ceptive; he has great delicacy of manner; he is a man of taste. He has, indeed, as Isabel recognizes, made the life of taste a vocation. "He had consulted his taste in everything—his taste alone per- haps, as a sick man consciously incurable consults at last only his lawyer: that was what made him so different from everyone else. Ralph had something of this same quality, this appearance of thinking that life was a matter of connoisseurship; but in Ralph it was an anomaly, a kind of humorous excrescence, whereas in Mr. Osmond it was the keynote, and everything was in harmony with it" (I, 377).

Isabel is warned against Osmond by Mrs. Touchett and Ralph, who attempt to persuade her that he is an idle poseur and a social parasite whose interest in her is purely venal. Both emphasize his inner emptiness. "There's nothing of him," says Mrs. Touchett. In a burst of frankness Ralph tells her that she was "meant for something better than to keep guard over the sensibilities of a ster- ile dilettante." Isabel turns a deaf ear to these warnings. The fal- lacy that causes her to overestimate Madame Merle causes her to overestimate Gilbert. Because he is the most refined and discrimi- nating man she has ever met, she assumes he must be the most virtuous. Opposition only strengthens her faith in him. She conceives of him as a dedicated man who has devoted himself with complete self-abnegation and with complete disregard of pecuniary values to the ideal of the civilized life. She regards him as a martyr to the cause of civility and culture, and she converts his most obvious defects into tantamount virtues. Her reply to Ralph's critique is a glowing and impassioned tribute:

> Do you complain of Mr. Osmond because he's not rich? That's just what I like him for. I've fortunately money enough; I've never felt so thankful for it as today. There have been moments when I should like to go and kneel down by your father's grave: he did perhaps a better thing than he knew when he put it into my power to marry a poor man—a man who has borne his poverty with such dignity, with such indifference. Mr. Osmond has never scrambled or struggled—he has cared for no worldly prize. If that's to be narrow, if that's to be selfish, then it's very well. I'm not frightened by such words, I'm not even displeased; I'm only sorry that you should make a mistake. Others might have done so, but I'm surprized that you should. You might know a gentleman when you see one—you might know a fine mind. Mr. Osmond makes no mistakes! He knows everything, he understands everything, he has the kindest, gentlest, highest spirit" (II, 73) .

Isabel's initially favorable impression of Gilbert is enhanced by his whole approach to her during his courtship. He is in love with her, however, as he is in love with his paintings or his Florentine villa. He regards her as a potential ornament—a rare trophy that he can display to an envying world. He is a narcissist. He expects Isabel to reflect his opinions and play the part of an admiring echo. His love, if love it can be called, is the purest egotism and the most refined solipsism, the offspring of vanity rather than of passion. Yet this very absence of passion gives him a tactical advantage in his dealings with Isabel. Unlike Lord Warburton and Caspar Goodwood, he never overwhelms her; he insinuates himself into her affections by slow degrees. He appeals to her as a person rather than as a woman. He talks to her about art, about life, about the predicament of the expatriated American. His tone of weary irony has the fascination of an oblique bid for sympathy, and Isabel is flattered to think that her sympathy is of value to a person so intricate. His proposal is uttered with the reticence and self-depreciation of a man whose main anxiety is not to intrude on her privacy and whose respect for her transcends sexual passion. It is precisely because she considers herself respected rather than desired that she banishes all qualms and decides to surrender.

In Isabel's eyes, Gilbert Osmond is the answer to her need to dedicate herself completely to the cause of a perfect *modus vivendi*, which now takes on the aspect of a supremely satisfying personal relationship with a man whom she regards as perfection incarnate. She recognizes the fallacy of her former conception of herself as morally and spiritually self-sufficient. Confronted at every turn with the fancied superiority of Gilbert, she stands accused of her own inadequacy. In marrying Gilbert she is acknowledging her fundamental longing to shift the problems of her life to stronger shoulders than her own. Gilbert, she vainly believes, will be the means of achieving that sense of moral self-content that she equates with happiness.

The myth of civility is responsible for Isabel's idealization of Osmond; the romantic myth of reciprocity is responsible for her idealized conception of married life. She envisages a relationship in which each will co-operate in fulfilling the deepest needs of the other. "She could surrender to him with a kind of humility, she could marry him with a kind of pride; she was not only taking, she was giving" (II, 82). He is, she realizes, a lonely man and a poor man, and she is grateful that it is within her power to relieve both his loneliness and his poverty. She is delighted to have a fortune to fling at his feet, and she is delighted to think that she has found at last a justifiable use for her money. She is dedicating herself and her fortune to a man whom she regards as the personification of the civilized life, and what deeper satisfaction could she ask than to devote herself and everything she has to the glowing ideal of civility?

As Isabel confronts much later the bitter reality of her married life, during a solitary night-long vigil in front of a dying fire in a room of the Palazzo Roccanera, she sadly calls to mind her earlier vision. She remembers how naively she had expected her relationship with Gilbert to lead "to the high places of happiness, from which the world would seem to lie below one, so that one could look down with a sense of exaltation and advantage, and judge and choose and pity . . . . " She recalls how Gilbert had impressed her because he was "poor and lonely and yet that somehow he was noble," and how she had hoped to "launch his boat for him" and "be his providence." She remembers how she had considered him "better than anyone else," and she sadly recalls her elation when "the finest—in the sense of being the subtlest—manly organism she had ever known had become her property" (II, 189-194) .

III

In a series of chapters which stand as one of our greatest fictional records of a personal disillusion, James describes how Isabel is gradually forced to recognize the true nature of Osmond, the extent of his perfidy, and the complete failure of her marriage. "You were ground in the very mill of the conventional!" says the dying Ralph Touchett. His remark is a poignant comment on the irony implicit in her fate. She who marries Gilbert Osmond on the assumption that their marriage is to be so much more than a relationship rooted in convention is doomed to discover that her husband is a man for whom conventions are everything. Marriage turns out to be a mere form emptied of content and meaning.

With great skill James shows us how Isabel attempts to ward off her bitter knowledge about Osmond. She desperately tries to exonerate him from any responsibilty for their marital failure. She forces herself to be loyal to him even when she realizes in her heart that he is unworthy of it. Appalled as she is at Osmond's readiness to sacrifice Pansy to his own ambition, she stills her scruples and co-operates with Osmond to the extent of discouraging Edmund Rosier, Pansy's lover, and directing Pansy to obey her father. Although she refuses to forward Pansy's match with Lord Warburton, she tries not to stand in its way. She places herself, indeed, in a curiously ironic position. She who had married for love finds herself the advocate of a marriage of convenience.

Yet Isabel's fundamental honesty overrides her reluctance to see Osmond as he really is, and she realizes that it is useless to lie to herself. The air of the Palazzo becomes poisoned with his unwitting self-revelations. He shows himself to be a man who, beneath all his veneer, is self-centered, narrow, jealous, mean-spirited, and cruel. Isabel's reward for trying to adopt his point of view about Pansy is to be accused of trying to influence Lord Warburton against her stepdaughter. The shock of this insult is succeeded by shocks whose impact is equally great, and the latent conflict between huband and wife becomes completely overt when Osmond forbids Isabel to go to England to visit her dying cousin. He is as jealous of her friendship with Ralph as he is jealous of her friendhip with Lord Warburton. Absolutely incapable of doing justice to Isabel's loyalty, he believes that she and Ralph are leagued in mutual criticism of himself. "That's why you like him—because he hates me," he tells her, and no words could express more vividly the abyss that has opened out between them.

As James traces the slow growth of Isabel's disillusion, one receives the impression that she regards it as almost incredible that a man of such discrimination and sensibility should be so base. She is bewildered rather than morally outraged, and her bewilderment is entirely comprehensible. In Osmond, after all, she is not confronted with the simple case of a bad man whom she had previously considered a good man. She is confronted rather with a peculiarly vivid instance of human perversity. Osmond is a dilemma, a paradox. He is a superior man and at the same time an immoral man. He is still the representative of the graces and amenities of the civilized state. Indeed his representative value is now socially acknowledged: their Palazzo is a gathering place for the best European society. Her money, it is true, has made his success possible, but his success has not depended on money alone. Money has simply given him the opportunity he needed to exercise his gifts as a host, as a conversationalist, as a collector, as an artist in living. Yet this highly polished and urbane man who has won himself a place in the vanguard of the civilized élite is, as Isabel knows only too well, an egotist without the slightest trace of a moral conscience. "Under all his culture, his cleverness, his amenity, under his good-nature, his facility, his knowledge of life, his egotism lay hidden like a serpent in a bank of flowers" (II, 196).

Isabel had previously thought Osmond superior to crass worldly considerations. She now sees how wrong she had been. She recognizes him for what he is—a superior type of worldling. His dominating desire is to excite admiration and envy, and he is prepared to sacrifice anyone in order to fulfill it. Isabel has at least the consolation of not standing alone—both Pansy and Madame Merle are in varying degrees the victims of Osmond. He is a man whose only criterion in life is the opinion of society.

Isabel's loss of faith in Osmond is at the same time a loss of faith in what he represents—civility. Her realization that the most civilized man she has ever known is at the same time the most predatory and the most self-centered has all the force of a tragic disillusion. Her earlier equation of civility and virtue is now replaced by a bitter insight. She realizes that the highly civilized man is not the most trustworthy but the least trustworthy of men. The civilized man, in other words, whose moral sensitivity one would tend to take for granted because of his finer human endowment, is most likely to be entirely lacking in moral sensitivity.

Isabel never displays herself to greater advantage than she does under the impact of this new knowledge. She impresses one as a noble soul confronted for the first time with the ignobility, the contrariety, the paradoxicality of man. She is saddened rather than embittered, disappointed rather than aggrieved. She indulges in no recriminations against Osmond, and the extent of her revenge against his accomplice, Madame Merle, is to refrain from taking any revenge. "Be a little easy and natural and nasty; feel a little wicked, for the comfort of it, once in your life," pleads the Countess Gemini after telling Isabel how she has been "framed," so to speak, by Osmond and Madame Merle. Isabel's reaction to the outrage perpetrated against her is not to feel wicked, however, but to feel sorry for the perpetrators. On learning that Madame Merle is Pansy's mother she exclaims: "And how the poor woman must have suffered at seeing me—!" (II, 371).

Osmond destroys both Isabel's illusions about the moral basis of civility and her illusions about the possibility of true reciprocity. She who had given herself in a spirit of "inspired and trustful passion" finds that her gift is absolutely unappreciated. Osmond neither loves her nor respects her. On the contrary, he finds her repellent. Her enthusiasms bore him. He is, indeed, as disillusioned with Isabel as she is with him. He is furious to discover that Isabel is unwilling to play the part of an admiring echo. She has, he recognizes with irritation, a distinct personality of her own with its own needs and claims—a personality, moreover, which because of its finer moral sensibility is in diametrical opposition to his own. His disappointment is expressed in an aloof contempt far more cruel than any overt criticism.

Isabel, who had at one time so blithely embraced the prospect of a life without emotional attachments, discovers through the debacle of her marriage the true meaning of isolation. She lives in the same house with Osmond, but she is completely separated from him. Rejected and spurned, she is flung back on herself, and she realizes that it is with herself that she must always live. She has moments when she is almost overcome by her situation. "She sat in her corner, so motionless, so passive, simply with the sense of being carried, so detached from hope and regret, that she recalled to herself one of those Etruscan figures couched upon the receptacle of their ashes." She has the slight consolation of hoping that the sharp edge of her present suffering will be blunted with the passing of time, but from her present perspective her future presents itself as a long, gray unalleviated vista too hideous to contemplate. "She should never escape; she should last to the end. Then the middle years wrapped her about again and the grey curtain of her indifference closed her in" (II, 391-393).

The only positive compensation that Isabel receives is the warm though belated understanding that she reaches with her cousin Ralph. As he lies upon his deathbed, she appreciates for the first time the extent and the depth of his love for her, and she pours into his sympathetic ear the story of the unadulterated misery of her marriage. He attempts as far as he may to minister to her suffering. "I don't believe that such a generous mistake as yours can hurt you for more than a little," he tells her, and he begs her to remember "that if you've been hated you've also been loved. Ah but, Isabel—*adored*!" It is, however, Ralph himself who has adored her, and Isabel recognizes his adoration too late. His death underlines and emphasizes her aloneness.

The strongest propulsive force in Isabel's nature had been the longing to transcend the limitations of the self, and Gilbert had suggested the possibility of such transcendence by means of a completely reciprocal personal relationship. This she no longer believes. She never for a moment considers that she might have been more successful had she married a different man; she never for a moment considers that she might be successful in establishing such a relationship in the future. She now recognizes the idea of the perfectly reciprocal relationship as a myth. In surrendering this myth, however, she is also acknowledging her own predicament, which is essentially tragic. It is the predicament of one who is doomed to live with the self that she longs to surrender.

Why, it may be asked, should Isabel regard herself as irredeemably alone? She has failed to establish an ideally satisfactory relationship, but this is no reason why she should not pitch her flag a little lower and make an intelligent compromise. Caspar Goodwood is, as always, ready and waiting, and only too anxious to take charge of Isabel's future. Abetted by Henrietta Stackpole, he passionately urges her to leave Osmond. There is, it may be argued, no reason why Isabel should not look forward to some fairly satisfactory relationship either with Caspar Goodwood or with someone like him.

The counsel of compromise has, however, no attractions for Isabel. She flees from Caspar's passionate embrace, not because she is frightened of his sexual ardour, but because she refuses to accept a relationship that must as a matter of course be a travesty of her original ideal of what a personal relationship should be. She prefers to face her aloneness without alleviations that must inevitably turn out to be vain. She takes spiritual satisfaction in confronting all the personal implications of her refuted idealism, and she should, in consequence, be praised for her honesty rather than criticized for her irrationality.

Isabel's decision to return to Osmond has excited a considerable amount of critical comment.[4] Some attribute it to a false sense of pride that refuses to admit a mistake before the world; others attribute it to an exaggerated sense of the sanctity of the marriage bond; others, more chivalrously, attribute it to a sense of loyalty to Pansy. They all concur, however, in regarding it as a mistake, and they are all, like Henrietta Stackpole, on the side of separation, divorce,' and remarriage. Why, they ask, should Isabel so perversely resume the misery of her married life with Osmond?

The assumption that in returning to Osmond, Isabel is returning to a life of misery is, I consider, a mistake. Isabel's disillusion was the cause of her unhappiness, and her disillusion is now complete. She is protected now by her own disenchantment. Osmond has done his worst—he has no more power to hurt or wound her. This consideration permits us to examine the motives for her decision in a new light.

Isabel's decision to return to Osmond should be interpreted in the light of her tragic consciousness. She is a woman who has learned that civilized life is composed of conventions that are as often as not mere masks thinly disguising egotism, selfishness, and immorality. The convention of marriage, the most central of human conventions, is frequently enough—as she has discovered through bitter personal experience—a facade concealing mutual incompatibility. The conventions of civility represent, she has found, little more than a sophisticated form of worldliness. Such is society, such is the world, and it is a world, moreover, in which it is impossible to find any truly deep personal satisfaction. It is, nevertheless, imperative to reconcile oneself to conventions in order to live in the world at all. It is the recognition of this that prompts her to return to her husband. She is resuming her place in conventional society. Hers, however, is the tragic consciousness of one who must be forever alienated from the conventions amongst which she is doomed to live.

IV

The Portrait of a Lady, then, is a study in disenchantment. It is the story of a young woman whose bitter personal disappointment opens her eyes to the chasm that separates what is real from what is ideal. Her tragic consciousness springs from her realization that her earlier ideals of life are irrelevant to the world as it is. Her ideals, in fact, sink to the level of myths.

It would be absurd to talk of tragic consciousness if Isabel's original ideals represented nothing more than the ingenuous pipe dreams of an inexperienced young girl. In this case her disenchantment would be a matter for rejoicing. We would simply say that she had grown up. It has been shown, however, that her earlier ideals are such as to command respect. In this sense, they have a certain universality of reference. They are ideals that were related to all that was noble in Isabel's temperament, and they are ideals that, one feels, should hold good if human life was as it ought to be. Their refutation is, in fact, an indictment of human life.

Isabel's dream of a completely satisfying personal relationship is one of the recurrent dreams of mankind. The longing for such a relationship is not, as James shows in this novel, necessarily related to cheap romantic egotism. In Isabel's case it is primarily a longing for moral and spiritual satisfaction and for self-transcendence, and it is as such related to the quest for the good life. It presupposes a readiness to give as well as to receive—self-transcendence is intimately associated with self-sacrifice.

Isabel's belief that Osmond is the man to fulfill this dream should not be written off as a pitiful instance of provincial stupidity. It is a belief inspired by an ideal of civilized life that has the highest degree of moral plausibility—an ideal, moreover, that has had wide historical distribution. It is an ideal that represents the moral demand that society at its best should be composed of the best types of men. If civilization has any valid moral meaning, it is only natural to infer—as Isabel does—that the "most civilized man in the world" should be the man most likely to respond to a deep personal appeal.

As Isabel discovers, however, the real world is one in which her ideals have no valid currency. It is, in consequence, a stripped and denuded world—where the cry for reciprocity must forever be denied; where what is most fair-appearing is at the same time the most treacherous. This is what she learns as a result of her marriage to Gilbert Osmond.

Some Grail Motifs in Eliot's "Prufrock"

by
Thomas C. Rumble

OF ALL OF T. S. Eliot's poems, *The Waste Land* and "The Love Song of J. Alfred Prufrock" have been most widely read and most frequently written about, primarily, I think, because critics and the editors of anthologies have seen in these two poems similarities in method, imagery, tone, theme, and structure which to a very great extent indicate that they are mutually complementary. The "Prufrock" poem, of course, is literally a "love song," however abortive and frustrated its conclusion; and at this literal level its speaker's object, as one writer has put it, "is to declare himself to a lady."[1] But most readers will sense that Eliot's intention in the poem is a great deal more serious than simply this. One can scarcely escape feeling, for example, that the plight of the single person speaking in the poem is meant somehow to represent in much more universal terms the plight of the society which produced him. And in the quiet terror of the whole, Eliot's abhorrence of this universal social plight shows through every image, every line. What I wish to propose here is a reason why the "Prufrock" and *The Waste Land* should seem so perfectly to complement each other; for, as I see it, the two poems represent respectively the germination and the fruition of a parable that Eliot hoped would serve as a vehicle for his early criticism of the state of the world in which he lived and wrote.

Critics have regularly called attention to Eliot's use of the Grail legend in *The Waste Land,* but they have all too often implied,

95

at least, that his knowledge of that legend derives almost wholly from Jessie L. Weston's book *From Ritual to Romance*.[2] It has apparently gone without notice that the "Prufrock" poem, written considerably earlier than either *The Waste Land* or *From Ritual to Romance*, suggests strongly that Eliot had already become preoccupied with the basic motifs of the Grail story and with the possibility that these motifs might provide precisely the kind of "objective correlative" he needed in order to express what he saw as the essential sterility afflicting his own age. But before turning to the "Prufrock" and to what seems to me Eliot's implicit but consistent and systematic use of the Grail motifs in that poem, and in order properly to orient the following discussion, let me summarize very briefly one version of the Grail legend—although I shall want later to point to certain elements of variant versions which are also relevant.

The "Prufrock" poem seems most closely related to the earliest versions of the Grail quest—those versions, that is, which center the story around the figure of Gawain. Among these is Heinrich von dem Turlîn's *Diu Crône*, which is, to utilize Jessie Weston's description of it, "a long, rambling poem, devoted to the praise of Gawain, and containing a mass of tradition relating to that hero, parts of which are, undoubtedly, of very early origin."[3] In the Grail episode of Heinrich's poem, Gawain comes to the castle of the Grail King in the company of Lancelot and Calogreant. The three knights are promised shelter for the night and are led to the elaborate and rose-strewn chamber of the Grail King, who, dressed in a gold-embroidered white robe, invites them to take part in the annual ceremony of the Grail feast. Gawain is seated next to the Grail King and slightly above his two companions. The knights are offered wine, but, having previously been warned, Gawain refuses to drink. Lancelot and Calogreant drink, however, and are promptly cast under a sleeplike spell. The Grail procession then enters, consisting most importantly of two youths, who carry a bleeding lance, and six weeping maidens, the most beautiful of whom carries the Grail vessel itself and is recognized by Gawain as the maiden who had previously warned him not to drink of the wine he would be served and not to fail to ask the meaning of the procession. Gawain asks this crucial question of the

Grail King, and immediately the entire assemblage rises with shouts of rejoicing. The king then explains that he and his people have existed for years in a state of life-in-death, and that, in asking this particular question, Gawain has achieved the quest of the Grail and has thus restored life to a dead people, fertility to a waste land. With the end of the king's explanation, and with the coming of dawn, the king, the Grail, and the entire company vanish; and as though waking from a dream, Gawain finds himself left in this rich hall by the sea with only his two companions and the six maidens of the Grail procession. The maidens, it is explained, had been the only persons alive in this barren realm; their duty had been, by command of God, to perform the Grail ceremony once each year until such time as the king and his land were restored to life and fruitfulness.[1]

As I have said, this outline represents but one of several different versions of the Grail story. But there are certain constant elements which are important. In all versions, for example, the central motif is that of quest and question. In all versions the Grail itself is in some way symbolic of the source and meaning of life. In all versions, through asking or failing to ask some critical question concerning the Grail, a knight restores or fails to restore to life a dead or wounded king and his sterile land.

It seems to me that Eliot's "Prufrock" is a poem which, through sometimes direct and sometimes inverse and ironic parallels of both motif and imagery, constitutes a kind of modern parable of this legend. We know, of course, that this is true, and more explicitly so, of his longer and later poem *The Waste Land*. But there is no mistaking the state of affairs in the "Prufrock" poem; the world in which its speaker moves is just as surely a "waste land" as is the world of Tiresias and Madame Sosostris, Mr. Eugenides and the Phoenician Sailor. With its

> . . . certain half-deserted streets,
> The muttering retreats
> Of restless nights in one-night cheap hotels
> And sawdust restaurants with oyster-shells (11. 4-7),

this is just as surely an "unreal city" as is that in which

A rat crept softly through the vegetation
Dragging its slimy belly on the bank
While I was fishing in the dull canal
On a winter evening round behind the gashouse.[5]

The opening lines of the "Prufrock" poem function as a statement of intent. They are spoken by Prufrock not as an introduction to a dramatic monologue or a soliloquy, as some have thought, but as the beginning of a "debate between body and soul," which, to my mind, best describes the entire structure of the poem. The opening lines involve the central motif of the Grail story; they concern both quest and question. And in the metaphorical comparison which they embody of evening and "a patient etherized upon a table," they incorporate incidentally an image that brings to mind a vision of a sterile land and its people, both of which are represented symbolically in the Grail legend by the Fisher King, who, "like a patient etherized," lies maimed or in a state of life-in-death upon his bier:

Let us go then, you and I,
When the evening is spread out against the sky
Like a patient etherized upon a table;
Let us go through certain half-deserted streets,
. . . . (. . . . .
Streets that follow like a tedious argument
Of insidious intent
To lead you to an overwhelming question. . . .
(ll. 1-4, 8-10)

Immediately following these opening lines, we find ourselves in a mock Grail chamber. The transition is an abrupt one, but the scene is nevertheless easily recognized; for the trivial, "hyper-cultivated chit-chat"[6] of the women who "come and go / Talking of Michelangelo" stands in ironic contrast to the serious and ceremonial procession of the weeping Grail maidens. And we learn shortly (l. 34) that this is a place of "the taking of a toast and tea," the imagery here doubling upon itself to suggest not only the actual scene and its ironic counterpart, the chamber of the

Grail feast, but, even more ironically, the scene of a Christian ritual of Holy Communion.

Once this abrupt shift of scene is accomplished, once we are inside this mock chamber of the Grail procession, Eliot intensifies his metaphor, for the following stanza forces upon us a progressively terrifying awareness of the essential sterility and lifelessness of the land into which we have come. Strangely enough, the central image of this stanza seems at first one of fertility; it involves the surrounding "yellow fog" which, catlike, "rubs its back upon the window panes," and the "yellow smoke" which, catlike, "rubs its muzzle on the window panes."[7] But we see immediately that this cat image is, after all, a symbol only of a potential fertility, a fertility which, frustrated, leaves us all the more conscious of the barrenness of our surroundings; for the yellow fog and yellow smoke

> Licked its tongue into the corners of the evening,
> Lingered upon the pools that stand in drains,
> Let fall upon its back the soot that falls from chimneys,
> Slipped by the terrace, made a sudden leap,
> And seeing that it was a soft October night,
> Curled once about the house, and fell asleep (ll. 17-22) .

The poem now turns to Prufrock's dilemma, to his "debate between body and soul." Does he dare ask the "overwhelming question"—dare "disturb the universe" by restoring to life this trivial and sterile world of his?[8] It is a matter to be pondered, and he rationalizes his indecision by telling himself again and again that there will be time to ask the question, time "to murder" what is and "to create" in its place what should be:

> . . . time for all the works and days of hands
> That lift and drop a question on your plate;
> Time for you and time for me,
> And time yet for a hundred indecisions,
> And for a hundred visions and revisions,
> Before the taking of a toast and tea.[9]

Prufrock's rationalization takes still another turn. Like the knight of every version of the Grail story, he wonders why it should have been given especially to him to put the "overwhelming question." In Prufrock's mind the argument is at once simple and convincing: since he himself has been for so long so much a part of this wasteland existence, why should it suddenly be his to presume to judge it, to put a question that will disturb it? Of the things which typify that existence he says,

> ... I have known them all already, known them all:
> Have known the evenings, mornings, afternoons,
> I have measured out my life with coffee spoons;
> I know the voices dying with a dying fall
> Beneath the music from a farther room.
> So how should I presume?

Nor is Prufrock's reluctance to presume the whole of the matter. Of this world himself, he must condemn this world; and his doing so, his finding "strength to force the moment to its crisis," will thus imply an inconsistency which, in the eyes of a world unwilling to be restored to life, must amount to a false and hypocritical self-martyrdom. For, as he says, he has also "known the eyes already, known them all"—

> The eyes that fix you in a formulated phrase,
> And when I am formulated, sprawling on a pin,
> When I am pinned and wriggling on the wall,
> Then how should I begin
> To spit out all the butt-ends of my days and
>   ways? (11. 56-60)

Though it is purely a personal reaction, perhaps, and needs no insistence, the image of Prufrock "formulated, sprawling on a pin" suggests to me the juxtaposed and ironic use of still another Grail motif. It brings to mind the "bleeding lance" and the "dolorous stroke" of the Grail story, both of which are in most versions of the legend connected with Christ's death on the Cross and are thus clearly symbolic of the idea of martyrdom. In any event, Prufrock's debate now hinges upon whether he will sacrifice himself to disturb the universe—even for its own ultimate good. And almost as though he had reached his decision, Prufrock asks yet twice again: "How should I presume?"

Yet, having asked this question of himself, Prufrock is led to complicate the matter further. As though granting momentarily that he should presume, he brings himself to ask as well, "And how shall I begin?" And with this last question he forgets temporarily the negativism of his previous rationalization; for, however tentatively, he *does* begin. "Shall I say," he asks,

> ... I have gone at dusk through narrow streets
> And watched the smoke that rises from the pipes
> Of lonely men in shirt-sleeves, leaning out of windows?
> (11. 70-72)

But this is much too devious a way to bring him to the "overwhelming question." Obviously it will not do, not even to begin. And Prufrock breaks off abruptly to lapse again into defeat and indecision, to mutter despairingly,

> I should have been a pair of ragged claws
> Scuttling across the floors of silent seas.[10]

From this point in the poem Prufrock's debate consists chiefly of furnishing himself with justifiable reasons why he should not have "bitten the matter off with a smile, / . . . squeezed the universe into a ball / To roll it toward some overwhelming question." He has made one abortive and frustrated beginning, and has "seen the moment of (his) greatness flicker." And now he asks himself over and over again whether, after all, it would have been "worth while." Though he has seen his head " (grown slightly bald) brought in upon a platter," he is, he says, "no prophet," the imagery here suggesting not only the martyrdom of John the Baptist, but the bleeding head upon the dish which, in the ceremonial procession of one version of the Grail myth, is substituted for the Grail itself.[11] Neither, he reminds himself, is he "Prince Hamlet, nor was meant to be"; and with this allusion Eliot synthesizes the whole matter of the poem. Prufrock is not Prince Hamlet because, no matter with what agonies of vacillation, Hamlet is one who *does* find "strength to force the moment to its crisis." Moreover, Hamlet finds that strength through asking of himself the very question that lies at the heart of Prufrock's dilemma:

> Who would fardels bear,
> To grunt and sweat under a weary life,
> But that the dread of something after death,
> The undiscover'd country from whose bourn
> No traveller returns, puzzles the will
> And makes us rather bear those ills we have
> Than fly to others that we know not of?[12]

The question is a monumental one. Though it lies outside the context of the "Prufrock" poem, it nevertheless explains implicitly Prufrock's negative comparison of himself and Hamlet. Even further, in terms of its parallels both of phrase and image, it is a question which connects with and suggests for the first time in the poem the full significance of the epigraph which Eliot quotes from Dante's *Inferno*. Questioned by Dante as to the reason for his punishment, and believing Dante also one of the dead, Guido da Montefeltro replies:

> If I thought that my answer were
> To a person who might return to the world,
> This flame-like tongue should remain still.
> But since never before from this depth
> Has anyone returned alive, if I hear truly,
> Without fear of scorn I answer you.[13]

Like Hamlet, Prufrock has by this point in the poem seen his "native hue of resolution" become

> . . . sicklied o'er with the pale cast of thought,
> And enterprises of great pitch and moment
> With this regard their currents turn awry,
> And lose the name of action.[14]

But unlike Hamlet, Prufrock is never able to resolve his "hundred indecisions," and in the end he turns from the contemplation of "some overwhelming question" to the trivial questions and decisions of his own trivial existence:

> I grow old . . . I grow old . . .
> I shall wear the bottoms of my trousers rolled. `
> Shall I part my hair behind? Do I dare to eat a peach?
> I shall wear white flannel trousers, and walk upon the beach
>   (11. 120-123) .

He has failed to seize his "moment of greatness"; his quest has been in vain. And like the knights who in most versions of the Grail quest fail, Prufrock now awakens by the sea, the weeping maidens of his vision, now suddenly turned mermaids, silently remonstrating his failure: "I have heard the mermaids singing, each to each," he says; "I do not think that they will sing to me." And again like the Grail knights who fail in their quests, Prufrock is now moved to comment bitterly upon his experience and to reflect with chagrin upon the failure both of body and of soul:

> We have lingered in the chambers of the sea
> By sea-girls wreathed with seaweed red and brown
> Till human voices wake us and we drown.[15]

All the World a Stage: The Elements of Drama in the Poetry of E. E. Cummings

by
Bernard Benstock

ON SEVERAL OCCASIONS in his career as a poet E. E. Cummings has demonstrated an interest in expressing himself as a dramatist, in creating characters and situations for the stage. His expressionistic play *Him*, his ballet *Tom*, and his "morality play" *Santa Claus* are indications of a dramatic inspiration, an eye for characterization, an ear for dialogue, a consciousness of interrelationships of individuals resulting in heightened situations, although each marks a departure from conventional drama and reveals the "touch of a poet" in the theater. Cummings' account of his experiences in French prisons when he was mistakenly imprisoned during World War I, *The Enormous Room*, is rather unique as an almost plotless prose work primarily devoted to fascinating character sketches of the inmates. The poet's other prose work, *Eimi*, an account of his trip to the Soviet Union in the early thirties, contains equally dramatic material—so much so that Cummings has included the Lenin's Tomb scene in the Caedmon recording of readings from his work.

Not only in these efforts, however, has Cummings demonstrated his theatrical touch; throughout the ten volumes of poetry published between 1923 and 1950 a keen sense of the dramatic has been apparent, particularly in the characterizations he has created. These "people" seem to provide a strong basis of reality in what is usually considered rather difficult poetry; they are an an-

104

chor of stability and rapport between poet and reader to prevent the poet's "flight of fancy" from completely ascending into the stratosphere of obscurity. If a decline in poetic power is observed in Cummings' later poetry, perhaps it is due not merely to sur- face obscurities (grammatical machinations, typographical eccen- tricities, tortured rhetoric), but also to the underlying loss in the poems of the forties and fifties of the poet's inherent sense of characterization. People and places are of greater importance in *Tulips and Chimneys* (1923), *&* (1925), *Xli Poems* (1925), *is 5* (1926), *W* [*ViVa*] (1931), *No Thanks* (1935), and *New Poems* (1938) than in *50 Poems* (1940), *1x1* (1944), and *Xaipe* (1950).

The constant drama which is enacted in many of the earlier poems, and in some of the later ones, is set against the scenic back- drop of Paris, New York, and the Boston-Cambridge area, prob- ably in that order of importance. It is Paris particularly that pro- vides the stage for many of Cummings' dramatic involvements— love affairs, the awakening of youth, even political imbroglios. In *&*, the reader finds himself often in the "bon cul de Paris" (97)[1] or, as in Post Impression XIV:

> (Fields Elysian
>
> the like,a) slEEping neck a breathing a   , lies
> (slo wlythe wom an pa)ris her
> flesh:wakes
>   in little streets . . . (84).

Disguised as a "WomanSellingBalloonS" (84), drowsily awaken- ing at dawn after the sleep of forgetfulness in the Champs Elysées (and hidden in the equally drowsy typography of the poetic page), Paris emerges as the opening scene in Cummings' perpetual drama. The poet repeatedly sets the same stage, relives the same Parisian street scene, and identifies himself with the landscape of this "lovecity":

> if to the colour of midnight
> to a more than darkness (which
> is myself and Paris and all
> things) . . . (75).

But nowhere in this early volume does Cummings depict Paris more graphically than in Post Impression V:

> Paris: this April sunset completely utters
> utters serenely silently a cathedral
> before whose upward lean magnificent face
> the streets turn young with rain ... (75-76) .

Here time and place are recorded in the dramatist's initial stage direction to the audience: the scene is Paris, the time is April. The association of Paris and April has become classic (and of course a cliché), existing with equal case in Tin Pan Alley ballads—the E. Y. Harburg-Vernon Duke "April in Paris" is an obvious case in point—and the poetry of the arch anti-sentimentalist, E. E. Cummings. To Cummings the association is a personal one, and constantly a fresh, vivid stimulus, although he is usually extremely careful to disguise his sentiment in typographical obscurity, in punning:

> to repass where
> flesh is heiry montparnasse
> is goosed by raspail ... (290)

or in actual jeering:

> So this Paris.
> i will sit in the corner and drink thinks and think drinks,
> in memory of the Grand and Old days ...
>
> what's become of Maeterlink
> now that April's here? (170)

April is the time regardless of the setting. Other months casually provide an occasional poem, but April runs through Cummings' poetry as a constant motif: in the form of noun, adjective, or even verb, April becomes a time, a place, a person, a state of being, a way of life. In the first poem of the first volume (the Epithalamion of *Tulips*) , we find:

And still the mad magnificent herald Spring
assembles beauty from forgetfulness
with the wild trump of April . . . (4) .

In "Puella Mia," we meet:

my very frail lady drifting
distinctly, moving like a myth
in the uncertain morning, with
April feet like sudden flowers . . . (14) .

April becomes the embodiment of feminine beauty, of the poet's
love: "thy body to me is April/in whose armpits is the approach
of spring . . . " (25) The "fingers of April" (40) and "April darkness" (54) are constant manifestations of the love motif dominant
in the early poems and never completely dormant throughout
Cummings' poetry. The motif perhaps reaches its ecstatic zenith
in the last poem of *is 5*, the last lines of which exclaim:

lady through whose profound and fragile lips
the sweet small clumsy feet of April came

into the ragged meadow of my soul (219) .

Even in one of the last poems of the most recent volume, the poet
maintains the ecstacy of the poetic exclamation of April and love:
"—it's april (yes, april; my darling) it's spring!" (465) .

But Paris and love do not always provide the scene, even if
April is the most popular time for the setting of Cummings'
poems. There's April in New York and Boston as well, and favorite settings for several poems during the mid-twenties are a Greek
restaurant and a Turkish coffee shop. Portrait II of *Xli Poems*
sets the time and place:

one April dusk the
sallow street-lamps were turning
snowy against a west of robin's egg blue when
i entered a mad street whose

mouth dripped with slavver of
spring

chased two flights of squirrel-stairs into
a mid-victorian attic which is known as
O ΠΑΡΘΕΝΩΝ . . . (143) .

The Parthenon, or some place very much like it, also provides the
setting for Sonnet XIII of the same volume, which begins: "when
i am in Boston, i do not speak./ and i sit in the click of ivory
balls. . . " (158) . The highlight of the scene merely offers a single
glance into the establishment where

> a waiter cleverly lugs
> indigestible honeycake to men
> . . . . one perfectly smooth coffee
> tasting of hellas, i drink, or sometimes two
> remarking cries of paklavah meeah (153) .

But this is a very different Boston scene from the one which is
taking place across the Charles River. There another sort of
drama is being enacted, and Cummings, the poet who fled the
pomp and circumspection of Cambridge society to enjoy the mud
of war-torn France, the Rive Gauche delights of postwar Paris,
and finally the Bohemian life of New York's Greenwich Village,
pulls back the curtain on

> the Cambridge ladies who live in furnished souls
> are unbeautiful and have comfortable minds
> (also, with the church's protestant blessings
> daughters, unscented shapeless spirited) . . . (58) .

One of the unscented, shapeless daughters of these Cambridge
ladies becomes a fascinating character in her own drama, a vignette which depicts her for an instant hopelessly divorced from
her comfortably safe Cambridge environs:

> "Gay" is the captivating cognomen of a Young Woman
>   of cambridge, mass.
> to whom nobody seems to have mentioned ye olde
>   freudian wish . . . (236) .

Miss Gay is entertained during her visit to New York by being taken to the Bronx Zoo, an experience which turns out to be rather unfortunate, since the animals were "that day inclined to be uncouthly erotic/ more particularly the primates . . . " (237). Her companion escorts her back to the Y.W.C.A. after some quite frigidly formal conversation and considers himself able to breathe again once he has finally deposited her there. He sums up Miss Gay's encounter with the denizens of the zoo: "Miss Gay had nothing to say to the animals and the animals had nothing to say to Miss Gay . . . " (237). As Cummings had commented at the end of the preceding poem in *W*: "GOD SAVE THE UNCOMMONWEALTH OF HUMANUSETTS" (236).

The New York world is another important scene in Cummings' perpetual poetic drama. His approach to the city is essentially panoramic; it spreads as a vast backdrop behind the small stage on which his people perform:

> at the ferocious phenomenon of 5 o'clock i find myself
> gently decomposing in the mouth of New York. Bet-
> ween its supple financial teeth deliriously sprouting
> from complacent gums, a morsel prettily wanders
> buoyed on the murderous saliva of industry. the mor-
> sel is i (149).

The scene is downtown New York and the main character (the sole character, as he huddles on the tiny stage against the towering panorama looming above him) is the poet himself; the landscape curls about him and attempts to devour him: "Vast cheeks enclose me" (149). In contrast to this frightening relationship between the poet and the city are the last two sonnets of *Xli Poems*, where the poet sings the praises of the streets of New York; as Cummings' Paris-April-Love songs mirror a constant refrain from Tin Pan Alley, so do these poems reflect such ditties as "The Sidewalks of New York":

> by god i want above fourteenth
>
> fifth's deep purring biceps, the mystic screetch
> of Broadway . . .

> give me the Square in spring,
> the little barbarous Greenwich perfumed fake . . . (160).

Sonnet XV moves into the Lower East Side where "the well-fed L's immaculate roar looped/ straightens, into nearest distance" (159) and "through the bumping teem of Grand. a nudging froth/ of faces clogs Second . . . " (159)

An earlier Cummings poem rhapsodized on this polyglot section of New York, the melting-pot district of the late nineteenth and early twentieth centuries, where characters of many lands shared the crowded stage of the slum area, living unfamiliar lives amid the din of many foreign tongues:

> my eyes are fond of the east side
> as i lie asleep my eyes go into Allen street the dark
> long cool tunnel of raving colour, on either side the
> windows are packed with hardslippery greens and
> helplessbaby blues and stic-ky chromes . . . (81).

(Here the city-scape in the hands of the poet-set designer becomes a harlequinade.)

> if sometimes my eyes stay at home
> then my mouth will go out into the East side,my
> mouth goes to the peddlers . . .

> is there anything my ears love it's
> to go into the east Side in a. dark street a hur-
> DygurdY with thequeer hopping ghosts of child-
> ren. . . . .

> my,ears,go into Hassan's place . . . (81).

Hassan's in New York, like the Parthenon, is an important setting for the little dramas being daily enacted in Cummings' poetry. Cummings tells us that "It is necessary to find Hassan's Place/ by tiny streets shrugging with colour . . . " (112). The place itself is vividly described in Portrait VI of *Xli Poems*:

> it's just like a coffin's
> inside when you die,
> pretentious and
> shiny and
> not too wide . . . (146) .

From there the poet goes on to describe the paintings on the wall, the Sultan, a Gainsborough, a portrait of Mary Magdalene, until he arrives at the host himself, Hassan, whose drama of life this poem actually is:

> effendi drifts between
> tables like an old leaf
> between toadstools
> he is the cheerfulest of men
> his peaked head smoulders
> like a new turd in April . . . (147) .

Then Hassan announces that he is dying and offers his customer coffee.

Also immortalized as a setting for a Cummings poem is Mc-Sorley's Old Ale House, the famous New York landmark in existence for over a hundred years on East Seventh Street, just off Cooper Square, with a potbellied stove, sawdust-covered floors, serving only ale and allowing no women on the premises:

> i was sitting in mcsorley's   outside it was New
> York and beautifully snowing.

> Inside snug and evil.   the slobbering walls filthily
> push witless creases of screaming warmth chuck pil-
> lows are noise funnily swallows swallowing revolv-
> ingly pompous a the swallowed mottle . . . (78) .

These then are the places, this is the time; all this is program information which the audience hurriedly surveys before the curtain goes up. The drama itself is the important aspect of the poems, and particularly the characters who people the drama. A typical vignette can be chosen almost at random; poem V of *W*, for example. Place: Dragon Street. Time: a night in August. Characters (in order of appearance) : "i"—the hero; "she"—the heroine; a man named Jones; and a man named Smith. Curtain.

> myself,walking in Dragon st
> one fine August
> night,i just
> happened to meet
>
> "how do you do" she smiling
> said "thought you
> were earning your living
> or probably dead"
>
> so Jones was murdered by
> a man named Smith and
> we sailed on the
> Leviathan   (226) .

Fast curtain. It is a simple series of events: a chance meeting, exposition, interaction of characters, far-reaching consequences of their involvement, happy ending. It is a quick drama of life, seen in but the twinkling of an eye, and recreated in three stanzas of twelve lines, stripped bare of embellishments, embroideries, and description. Only time and place are given; dialogue develops the relationship of the primary characters, and a single piece of action resolves the plot. The slice of life thus presented is cut very thin (almost transparent) ; only a few deft strokes are used to sketch the characters.

Elsewhere throughout Cummings' poems events are sketched with similar austerity; only the characters are developed, for it is the people of Cummings' life-drama who are significant. What *happens* to them is only a subplot to the tragedy and comedy of their *being*. The range of characterization covers a wide gamut, for on his stage the poet allows many types of heroes and villains —and he is rarely vague about his own attitudes toward these people. Many a famous person will find himself strolling Cummings' stage, but might find it difficult recognizing himself in so strange a mask, performing so unfamiliar a role. The famous brush should-

ers on this stage with the obscure, the individual with the stereotype, the personified character with a name and identity of his
own and the expressionistic character with but a tag to identify
him to the audience.

Let us first examine the famous: they range from such impossible extremes as the well-known Western hero, William Cody—

> Buffalo Bill's
> defunct
>> who used to
>> ride a watersmooth-silver
>>> stallion. . . (50)

—to the Egyptian Queen Cleopatra:

> Cleopatra built
> like a smooth arrow or
> a fleet pillar is eaten
> by yesterday. . . (88) .

They strut along Cummings' stage shorn of all romance and glory
save the legend of their physical beauty, which, although the first
aspect of their existence to perish into dust, remains for the icono-
clastic poet the only permanent contribution they seem to make
to the history of civilization. About Cody, Cummings drolly comments:

>   Jesus
> he was a handsome man
>   and what i want to know is
>
> how do you like your blueeyed boy
> Mister Death (50) .

To Antony's paramour, the poet intones:

> and O My Lady Lady Of
> Ladies you
> who move beautifully in the winds
> of my lust. . . (91) .

Cummings' epitaph for former president Warren Harding is not nearly so flattering; despite his distinguished good looks, the deceased president goes unmourned with this sort of irreverent eulogy:

> the only man woman or child who wrote
> a simple declarative sentence with seven grammatical
> errors "is dead"
> beautiful Warren Gamaliel Harding
> "is" dead. . . (242) .

Painters and sculptors fare better under Cummings' spotlights than do the fellow writers who share his stage with them. Aristide Maillol is celebrated as an artist from whose

> soul comes
> a keen pure silence) such hands can
> build a (who are like ocean patient) dreams's
>
> eternity (you feel behind this man
> earth's first sunrise). . . (439) .

And Pablo Picasso is dubbed: "Lumberman of The Distinct/ . . . you hew form truly . . . " (144) . Many other modern painters become Cummings' set designers, presenting upon the stage of the poet's soul the visual image of his concept of beauty. Song II of *Xli Poems* celebrates several of them:

> of my
> soul a street is:
> prettinesses Pic-
> abian tricktrickclickflick-er
> garnished
> of stark Picasso
> throttling trees

hither
my soul
repairs herself with
prisms of sharp mind
and Matisse rhythms
to juggle Kandinsky gold-fish

away from the gripping gigantic
muscles of Cézanne's
logic. . . (133-134) .

In contrast to such praise for masters of the visual and plastic arts are Cummings' depictions of his fellow men of letters; Ernest Hemingway, for example, is epigrammatically dismissed with:

what does little Ernest croon
in his death at afternoon?
(kow dow r 2 bul retoinis
wus de woids uf lil Oinis (294) .

Bohemian Joe Gould, whose path crossed Cummings' many times during his saunterings through Greenwich Village with tobacco-streaked beard and cigarette holder, presumably collecting material for his one-million-word oral history of the world, is slightly more sympathetically treated in a poem in *No Thanks* which begins: "little joe gould has lost his teeth and doesn't know where/ to find them" (294) and ends with the couplet: "Amérique Je T'Aime and it may be fun to be fooled/ but it's more fun to be more to be fun to be little joe gould" (295) . Also easily recognized is poet-editor-anthologizer Louis Untermeyer in his epigram:

mr u will not be missed
who as an anthologist
sold the many on the few
not excluding mr u (394) .

And one of the longer "prose poems" in *is 5* manages to demolish several "classical" writers:

Kipling again H. G. Wells, and Anatole France
shooks hands again . . .

a water-
melon causes indigestion to William Cullen Longfellow's small negro son, Henry Wadsworth Bryant (188).

Irreverence for the great (or those the world at large considers
great) marks Cummings' special bitterness, reserved for incom-
petent persons in high places, for pomposity in general, and particularly for political demagogues and bullies. The technique of
scrambling names in order to express his refusal to accept the
legend of fame simply because history books have been lavish with
praise for America's heroes is used almost indiscriminately in
poem XIII of *W*, where American presidents from George Washington .to Calvin Coolidge are scurrilously presented; the poem
begins when

> remarked Robinson Jefferson
> to Injustice Taughed
> your story is so interested
> but you make me laft. . . (232-233).

and includes Wouldwoe Washington, Lydia E. McKinley, Buch,
Abe, Clever Rusefelt, Theodore Odysseus Graren't, and Coolitch.
    The villains and grotesque characters who parade across the
boards in Cummings' poetry are numerous: they include politicians—"a politician is an arse upon/which everyone has sat except a man" (394); salesmen—"a salesman is an it that stinks
Excuse/Me" (394); and American tourists in Europe:

> mine eyes have seen
> the glory of
> the coming of
> the Americans . . .
> —the substantial dollarbringing virgins . . . (183).

Also among these bit-players one finds the poet's uncles:

> my uncle
> Daniel fought in the civil
> war band and can play the triangle
> like the devil . . .
>   my uncle Tom
> knits and is a kewpie above the ears . . . (181) .

Only Uncle Sol is treated with a bit of sympathy, although he was "a born failure. . . " (173) . Poem X of the first part of *is 5* concerns Uncle's pathetic misadventures as a farmer and progresses through a comic series of farm ventures dependent upon the failure of his previous attempt—almost in Chaplinesque form of pratfall following pratfall—until the final denouement of Uncle Sol's suicide which "started a worm farm" (174) . Cummings is aware here that to the playwright pathos is closer to comedy than to tragedy, and many of his character sketches border on the pathetically comic. One cannot help feeling, however, that Cummings' characterization of Jews and Negroes relies heavily on the grotesque stereotype. In many poems, one finds only the broad lash of caricature, as in such portraits as:

> a kike is the most dangerous
> machine as yet invented
> by even yankee ingenu
> ity. . . (454)

or:

> one day a nigger
> caught in his hand
> a little star no bigger
> than not to understand. . . (442) .

His poems of New York include "pompous ancient jews" (159) against the backdrop of the Lower East Side, and wealthier Jews in better parts of town:

> IKEY (GOLDBERG) 'S WORTH I'M
> TOLD $ SEVERAL MILLION
> FINKELSTEIN (FRITZ) LIVES
> AT THE RITZ WEARS
> earl & wilson COLLARS (176) .

In poem IV of the fourth part of *is* 5, Cummings combines the caricatured Jew and the stereotyped Negro as they function as part of the over-all New York scene against which he himself as the poet moves:

> but if i should say
> goodmorning trouble adds
> up all sorts of quickly
> things on the slate of that
> nigger's
> face (but
>
> If i should say thankyouverymuch
>
> mr rosenbloom picks strawberries
> with beringed hands. . . (207) .

Cummings' portraits of Communists are not nearly so consistent. Although he caricatures the newspaper editorial's Moscow-financed puppet in poem 30 of *No Thanks*—

> (all good kumrads you can tell
> by their alturistic smell
> moscow pipes good kumrads dance)
> kumrads enjoy
> s.freud knows whoy
> the hope that you may mess your pance. . . (296)

—his sympathy is felt in an earlier poem in *is* 5 which describes the brutal breaking up of a Parisian Communist demonstration near the Arc de Triomphe by the French police:

there are 50 (fifty) flics for every
one (1) communist and
all the flics are very organically
arranged. . .

the
communists pick
up themselves friends
& their hats legs &

arms brush dirt coats
smile looking hands
spit blood teeth

the Communists have (very) fine eyes
(which stroll hither and thither through the
evening in bruised narrow questioning faces) (196-197).

This sort of inconsistency makes it difficult for the reader to piece
together a complete rationale concerning the poet's attitudes and
ideas, although certain prejudices and perspectives are rather apparent. Perhaps the one poem that best sums up Cummings' list
of "villains"—although it too has its ambiguities—is poem 22 of
No Thanks:

when muckers pimps and tratesmen
    delivered are of vicians
        and all the world howls stadesmen
            beware of politisions

                beware of folks with missians
                    to turn us into rissions
                    and blokes with ammunicions
                who tend to make incitions

                and pity the fool who cright
            god help me it aint no ews
        eye like the steak all ried
    but eye certainly hate the juse (292) .

The poet's antagonism for these individual characters becomes part of a broader pattern when it begins to include mankind in general. At least a dozen poems can be cited in which Cummings reveals a distinct repugnance for "people" in particular and "humanity" in general; they develop quite obviously from the individuals already presented, from the people around him, the characters he observes and judges. In the Preface to the 1938 edition of *Collected Poems*, Cummings distinguished between "You and I" and "mostpeople":

> The poems to come are for you and for me and are not for most-people—it's no use trying to pretend that mostpeople and our-selves are alike. Mostpeople have less in common with our-selves than the squarerootofminusone. YouandIare human beings;mostpeople are snobs (331).

Cummings' mass representation of "mostpeople" in his poetry is decidedly more scurrilous than this polite differentiation; in poem IV of part three of *is 5* they form the religious procession following a glass box containing the "exhumed/hand of Saint Ignatz" (201):

> sensuously
> the crowd
> howls faintly
> blubbering pointing. . . (201).

In poem 24 of *50 Poems*, people are depicted as barren of soul, mind, and heart (a vital triumvirate in Cummings' world, a trinity whose mystic unity is Love—see *Xaipe*, poems 23, 27, and 66); they are called the "socalled people" (366) and since they are devoid of the basic trinity composing the secret of love,

> all these hundreds upon thousands of
> people socalled if multiplied by twice
> infinity could never equal one. . . (336).

Even before the Preface to the 1938 volume, Cummings had creat-ed the theatrical personification called "mostpeople" in his verse. He outlined the inhibitions, restrictions, and repressions of this character, partly with sympathy and partly with condemnation in poem 29 of *No Thanks*:

> most (people
> simply
> can't)
> won't (most
> parent people musn't
> shouldn't) most daren't. . . (295) .

In poem 40 of *50 Poems*, they are dismissed as "a peopleshaped toomany-ness far too" (380) ; in poem 5 of *Xaipe*, they are "a loudness called mankind" (431) ; and in poem 22 of that volume, Cummings devotes the first twelve lines of a Shakespearean sonnet to deliver an ultimatum of conditions, while the closing couplet announces:

> then we'll believe in that incredible
> unanimal mankind (and not until)   (442) .

To what extent Cummings' vicious portrait of "mostpeople" is to be equated with a philosophic condemnation of mankind becomes apparent in several other poems in which "mankind" replaces the ambiguous "mostpeople" as the central character. In poem IV of *1 x 1*, he is "this busy monster,manunkind" (397), while in *W*, poem VII satirically celebrates:

> LONG LIVE that Upwardlooking
> Serene Illustrious and Beatific
> Lord of Creation,MAN. . . (227) .

As humanity in poem XLII of the same volume, he is relegated to the role of a "small/hoping insect,humanity" who "achieves/ (moult beyond difficult moult) amazing doom . . . " (253) . But the most definite statement—although it expresses an obvious ambivalence—appears in *Xli Poems*, where the poet comments on mankind's basic inconsistencies, hypocrisies, and self-deceptions:

> Humanity i love you because you
> are perpetually putting the secret of
> life in your pants and forgetting
> it's there and sitting down
>
> on it
> and because you are
> forever making poems in the lap
> of death Humanity
>
> i hate you (152).

The trinity of soul, mind, and heart again is denied prosaic mankind in poem IV of *1x1*, the first and last quatrains of which declare:

> of all the blessings which to man
> kind progress doth impart
> one stands supreme i mean the an
> imal without a heart.
> . . . .
> Without a heart the animal
> is very very kind
> so kind it wouldn't like a soul
> and couldn't use a mind (390-391).

But if these are the villains, Cummings has his heroes and heroines as well (presumably the "You and I" of the 1938 preface) ; specifically they are a myriad collection of unknown people characterized by their individuality and refusal to be herded into a mass. They may well be considered antisocial and undesirable by the *bourgeoisie*, but to E. E. Cummings they are real people, beautiful and defiant. They include the beggar in poem VI of *W* who pleads with a passerby for a handout, characterizing the distinction between himself and "mostpeople":

> Some
> people

```
's future is toothsome like
(they got
pockets full. . .

    mine's tou
ching this crump
led cap mumble some
thing. . . (226-227) .
```

Others are prostitutes like Marjorie—"in making Marjorie god
hurried/a boy's body on unsuspicious/legs of girl" (114) — or
Fran, Mag, Glad, Dorothy, Loretta, Alice, and Cecile, those "ir-
reproachable ladies firmly lewd" (109), or the Five Americans
(Liz, Mame, Gert, Marj, and Fran) who are the subjects of the
first five sonnets of part one of *is 5*, and all the others who work at
Dick Mid's, the Greenwich Village brothel that is the setting for
many a Cummings poem (see *Chimneys*, Sonnets-Realities IV, and
&, D, Sonnets-Realities XX) . Also, they are drunken Dorothy with
"her common purple/soul" (44), and dead Effie—"whose brains
are made of gingerbread" (95) —and the Parisian prostitutes of
Portrait XII of &, "A" (Mimi, Marie Louise Lallemand, Lucienne,
Manon, *et al.*) , and Jimmie who's "got a goil and/ she coitnly can
shimmie" (170), and the dead soldiers of World War I, Jock,
James, Will, and Harry (194), and even such thugs as the "buncha
hardboil guys frum duh A.C." (239) and "poets yeggs and thirs-
ties. . . " (186) . It is a veritable rogues' gallery of the outcast and
rejected, each of whom carries a shred of divinity; the Christ image
looms large in "a man who had fallen among thieves":

> Brushing from whom the stiffened puke
> i put him all into my arms
> and staggered banged with terror through
> a million billion trillion stars (184) .

The list of heroes includes children who are "petals/their song is a
flower" (377) and poets—"coward,clown,traitor,idiot,dreamer,
beast—/ such was a poet" (402) —and lovers:

> lovers are mindless they
> higher than fears are hopes
> lovers are those who kneel
> lovers are those whose lips
> smash unimagined sky
> deeper than heaven is hell (402) .

But a special group of freaks and outcasts form a strange corps of actors in Cummings' comic drama; they are an anachronistic group of little people whose sole function seems to be to serve as catalytic agents to engender the happiness of lovers and the delight of children. They include the circus performers of the second poem of *No Thanks*, the "fat strongman" (277) and lion tamer, the lamplighter of poem VI of part three of *is 5*—"touching the glass/boxes one by one with his magic/stick" (203), the knife sharpener who "sharpens say to sing" (443), the "mender/of things" of poem 62 of *Xaipe*, and especially the organ grinder of Post Impression V of *Tulips* whose "box sprouts/ fairies" (56), and the "little/lame balloonman" of the first of the Chansons Innocentes of the same volume who

> whistles   far   and wee
>
> and eddieandbill come
> running from marbles and
> piracies and it's
> spring
>
> when the world is puddle-wonderful. . . (21) .

Probably the most majestic hero in Cummings' world is the conscientious objector, Olaf; in almost epic fashion Cummings announces:

> i sing of Olaf glad and big
> whose warmest heart recoiled at war:
> a conscientious object-or. . . (244) .

Olaf emerges as a character of gigantic proportions, a tragic hero who refuses to accept the slogans and catchwords of American patriotism; remaining stalwart to his pacifistic ideals, Olaf defies the torture imposed upon him by the American military brass. He is brutally beaten and thrown

> into a dungeon, where he died
> Christ (of His mercy infinite)
> i pray to see;and Olaf,too
>
> preponderatingly because
> unless statistics lie he was
> more brave than me: more blond than you (244-245) .

An odd note is offered in Cummings' two poems about his own parents. Here the antisentimentalist reveals a graceful touch of sheer emotion, carefully avoiding an excess of obvious emotional feeling or the crass commercial sentiment of a Mother's Day or Father's Day card. He praises his mother in poem XLIII of *W*:

> if there are any heavens my mother will(all by herself)have
> one. It will not be a pansy heaven nor
> a fragile heaven of lilies-of the-valley but
> it will be a heaven of blackred roses. . . (253) .

Concerning his father, the poet is capable of remaining somewhat more vague in his sentiment, perhaps again displaying an ambivalence in keeping with his youthful attempt to break away from the parental fold in Cambridge and wallow in the mud of World War I France. Poem 34 of *50 Poems* begins with the quatrain:

> my father moved through dooms of love
> through sames of am through haves of give,
> singing each morning out of each night
> my father moved through depths of height (373) .

and closes seventeen stanzas later with:

and nothing quite so least as truth
—i say though hate were why men breathe—
because my father lived his soul
love is the whole and more than all (375) .

The most unusual aspect of Cummings' dramatis personae is
not so much his depiction of recognizable people, but his personification of abstract values. The discernible "mostpeople" more
often gives way to the abstract "noone," "nobody," "someone,"
and "anyone." In poem XIII of the fourth part of *is 5*, "Nobody
wears a yellow/flower in his buttonhole" (213) and in poem LIX
of *W*, "Nobody knows/ where truth grows. . . " (264). In both
cases "Nobody" is specifically capitalized. Elsewhere, poem 2 of
Xaipe, "Nobody" becomes "noone," the merging of the two words
into a single word transforming them into a single personification
like "mostpeople":

> noones
> are coming
> out in the gloam
> ing together are
> standing together... (429) .

And in poem VII of the N section of *&*, "nobody" is contrasted with
"everyone":

> we'd go up higher with all the pretty people
>
> than houses and steeples and clouds
> go sailing
> away and away sailing into a keen
> city which nobody's ever visited, where
> always
>   it's
>   Spring) and everyone's
> in love and flowers pick themselves (103) .

Here the words "nobody" and "everyone" can be read on a literal

level to have their exact semantic values—"nobody" referring to
an absence of people, "everyone" to a totality of people—but the
poem fits more closely into the Cummings pattern of personification when we accept "we" as the two lovers, the "pretty people"
as the cast of anachronistic little people (the circus performers,
balloon venders, knife sharpeners, etc.) , "nobody" as those people outside the pale—the prosaic who are incapable of accepting
beauty and imagination—and "everyone" as the "You and I" in-
group who are alive and aware. Another such "nobody" who cannot appreciate beauty is the "someone" of poem 45 of *No Thanks*:

> sometimes
>   in) Spring a someone will lie (glued
> among familiar things newly which are
> transferred with dusk)wondering why this star
> does not fall into his mind. . . (307) .

An entire cast is present in the "our town" family drama contained in poem 29 of *No Thanks*: the leading player is the nonentity of an individual named "anyone," who lacks real individuality
and is pathetically contrasted with the immenseness of the backdrop of the eternal seasons and the elements against which his
petty life is set:

> anyone lived in a pretty how town
> (with up so floating many bells down)
> spring summer autumn winter
> he sang his didn't he danced his did (370) .

"Anyone" marries—"someones married their everyones" (370) —
and lived his mediocre existence in his "pretty how town" until
he eventually died:

> one day anyone died i guess
> (and noone stooped to kiss his face)
> busy folk buried them side by side
> little by little and was by was. . .

noone and anyone earth by april
wish by spirit and if by yes (370-371) .

If this "pretty how" world of insignificant anyones and nobodies
is dull and dreamless, the broader expanse of Cummings' panorama is peopled by greater deities: the elements and the seasons of
the preceding poem appear often in drama of their own, a far
greater drama. Often they are capitalized into divine beings—the
sea, for example, in Sonnets-Unrealities II of *Chimneys,* takes
precedence as a divinity over God: the former is capitalized, the
latter remains in lower case letters:

> god gloats upon Her stunning flesh. Upon
> the reachings of Her green body among
> unseen things, things obscene . . . (61) .

In the sestet of the sonnet, Cummings declares: "god Is The Sea"
(61) . He has capitalized the initial letter of each word except
"god," and sums up this reversed deification as "god worships
God. . . " (62) .

The gender of these characters is not easy to determine; they
vary with the material of the individual poems. In poem I of
part four of *is 5,* the moon's gender is neuter at the outset—"the
moon looked into my window/it touched me with its small hands"
(205) —but becomes feminine before the poem is over: "the moon
smiled she/let go my vest. . . " (205) . She remains a woman in
poem XVIII of the same section—"now she sharpens and becomes
crisper" (216) —and in poem 18 of *50 Poems:* "she cannot read or
write,la moon" (362) . Rain and earth are male and female respectively in the sexual symbolism of the opening Epithalamion
of *Tulips,* with the sky as the rain's wife in the triangle:

> Thou aged unreluctant earth who dost
> with quivering continual thighs invite
> the thrilling rain the slender paramour
> to toy with thy extraordinary lust,
> (the sinuous rain which rising from thy bed

steals to his wife the sky and hour by hour
wholly renews her pale flesh with delight) . . . (3) .

Moon, Rain, Snow, Sea, Mountains, Time, Spring, April all
parade across the stage; each is an amorphous character capable
of assuming various disguises to be in character for a multitude of
dramatic situations, each changes sex, mask, costume, size, and
proportions to conform with the requirements of every new scene.

Besides the elements and the seasons, various other abstract con-
cepts become concrete characters in Cummings' work: Love is a
major figure, personified in poem LXVIII of *W*:

> love's also there:
> and being here imprisoned, tortured here
> love everywhere exploding maims and blinds
> (but surely does not forget,perish,sleep
> cannot be photographed,measured. . . (270) .

Fear is another such abstraction who assumes human proportions
to accept a role in Cummings' drama: "The big/fear Who held us
deeply in His fist. . . " (208) .

Even algebraic numbers and letters form a human equation on
the poet's stage; what is more dramatic than the eternal triangle?
Cummings graphically unfolds the drama of the conflict of the
two opposite angles of the base of that triangle in poem IX of *W*:

> y is a WELL KNOWN ATHLETE'S BRIDE. . .
> & z
> =an infrafairy of floating
> ultrawrists. . .
>
> and there was yz
> SHOT AND KILLED her
> (in his arms) Self
>   & Him. . . (228-229) .

The tragedy of the "2 boston/Dolls" (229) found dead in a hotel
bedroom is re-enacted here in terms of the algebraic values of y

and z, providing a mathematical detachment from the incident, an audience's aethetic distance from the immediacy of the action. In Portrait VIII of *Xli Poems*, five customers in the Boston Turkish coffee shop are depicted as a, b, c, x, and y: their interrelationships depend upon the participants in the backgammon game (x and y) being separated from the onlookers (a, b, and c) :

> a has gold
> teeth b pink
> suspenders c
> reads Atlantis
>
> x and y play   b
> cries "effendi" "Uh" "coffee" . . . (148) .

As distinct mathematical entities, each has his individuality, but as a formula they constitute "5 / derbies-with-men-in-them" (148) , since none is unique.

The most significant character in the entire realm of Cummings' dramatic world is Death—a character well depicted in his various guises and ramifications in the morality play, *Santa Claus*. Death's gender varies from poem to poem; he is masculine in sonnet XI of *Xli Poems*—"who's most afraid of death? thou/art of him/utterly afraid" (157) —and in Amores VI of *Chimneys*:

> if that he come receive
> him as your lover sumptuously. . .
>
> he is called death (36) .

He is addressed in the Buffalo Bill poem as "Mister Death" (50) , but is "Mrs. Death" (442) in poem 23 of *Xaipe* and "madame death" (381) in poem 43 of *50 Poems*. He is a deity in Song II of *Tulips*: "Death, Thee i call rich beyond wishing" (11) , and is the major figure in the dramatic triangle of poem XII of section A of &:

suppose
Life is an old man carrying flowers on his head.

young death sits in a café
smiling, a piece of money held· between
his thumb and first finger

(i say "will he buy flowers" to you. . .)

and my love slowly answered I think so. But
I think I see someone else

there is a lady, whose name is Afterwards
she is sitting beside young death, is slender;
like flowers (83) .

Here, as the conqueror of Life and paramour of Afterwards, Death
as a character has a major role in the dramatic struggle of the
poem. In many other Cummings poems that role is duplicated:
whether in contrast with Love—"death(having lost)put on his uni-
verse/ . . . Love(having found)wound up such pretty toys" (324) ;
or in contrast with beauty—"death,as men call him,ends what
they call men/—but beauty is more now than dying's when" (421) ;
or in a triangle with Love and Time—"i do excuse me, love, to
Death and Time" (154), Death emerges as a unifying force in
the dramatic struggle, a central character with a variety of facades,
a cloak of many colors, and a great performer's ability to change
his personality completely while on stage in order to portray the
widest range of experiences.

Death as the central figure presents the key to Cummings' world
of puppets. As in *Santa Claus*, the poetic realm of Cummings'
stage is essentially a medieval morality play, but the epical Every-
man (fostered by an omnipotent God and guided by his Good
Deeds into the Afterwards beyond Death) has given way to the
character of Death himself. "Mostpeople" is far too prosaic and
earth-bound a creature to be an epic character to Cummings; it
remains only for the abstract "villain" of the moral melodrama to
be transformed into a concrete hero, for Death as protagonist to
dominate Cummings' modern morality play.

The Individual and the Community: Faulkner's *Light in August*

by
James L. Roberts

I

LIGHT IN AUGUST is probably Faulkner's most complex and difficult novel. Here he combined numerous themes on a large canvas where many aspects of life are vividly portrayed. The publication of this novel marked the end of Faulkner's greatest creative period—in four years he had published five substantial novels and numerous short stories.[1] *Light in August* is the culmination of this creative period and is the novel in which Faulkner combines many of his previous themes with newer insights into human nature. In *Sartoris, The Sound and the Fury,* and *As I Lay Dying,* Faulkner had examined the relationship of the individual to his family. In his next major novel, *Absalom, Absalom!,* Faulkner returned to the family as the point of departure for his story. In *Light in August,* the family as a unit is replaced by the community, which although not examined as the family is in other novels, serves as the point of departure.

The novel may be interpreted on many levels. It suggests such themes as man's isolation in the modern world, man's responsibility to the community, the sacrifice of Christ, the search-for-a-father, man's inhumanity to man, and the theme of denial and flight as opposed to passive acceptance and resignation.[2] Each of these can be adequately supported, but none seems to present the whole intent of the novel. Perhaps this is because the complexity of the novel yields to no single interpretation but seems to require a multiple approach. The complex theme of man's need to live within himself while he recognizes his responsibility both to himself and to his fellow man will support such a multiple approach to *Light in August*. In terms of this general statement, the central metaphor is that of the circle, which is in turn supported by the general structure of the novel.

The circular image is first presented through Lena Grove. Both her curving shape and various circular images make this the dominant image throughout the novel.[3] She is "like something moving forever and without progress across an urn" (6).[4] The urn, then, is used symbolically in connection with Lena. It becomes symbolic of her enduring qualities and also is one of the many symbols that connect life with death since the urn is also used in burial rites. Thus, the endurance of Lena is correlated symbolically with the death of Joe Christmas.[5] Other images such as the wagon "like a shabby bead upon the mild red string of road," and the road like "measured thread being rewound onto a spool" (7) suggest the completeness with which Lena views life, and how she is fully immersed in a timeless world of natural surroundings. The final image of the first section is the circular column of smoke rising from Joanna Burden's house which again connects Lena to Joe Christmas' actions. Lena, therefore, with her earthy nature, seems to represent those qualities which will endure forever; and the circular images connected with her (and with the action in general) suggest Eccles. 1:4-6 "A generation goes, and a generation comes, but the earth remains forever. The sun rises and the sun goes down, and hastens to the place where it rises. The wind blows to the south, and goes round to the north; round and round goes the wind, and on its circuits the wind returns." Likewise, *Light in August* opens and closes with sections about Lena Grove. Structurally, therefore, the circular image is used to suggest connections between Joe and Lena, to bring out certain qualities for which Lena stands and to act as an encompassing frame for the whole novel. She is the outside frame for the whole novel and the outside frame of the wheel (circle) transversing all experience and centering on no particular or specific experience.

The Reverend Gail Hightower may be roughly compared to the spokes of the wheel, for through him the two strands of the novel are brought into a unity. Hightower is the moral reflector of the novel. He is introduced immediately following the Lena (and Byron Bunch) section, and his section immediately precedes the closing scene of the novel. If then, the center, or axle, of the novel is the Joe Christmas section, Hightower stands between the center and outside rim and connects the two. But Hightower is not just the moral reflector of the novel in the Jamesian sense; he must also be an active participant in the novel. He must gain and learn from his experience so that his life becomes meaningful at last and this meaning is pictured again by the circular image as Hightower's life and its meanings evolve slowly into significance through the magnificent "wheel" passage at the end of the novel. It is in this passage that Hightower's "thinking begins to slow now. It slows like a wheel beginning to run in sand, the axle, the vehicle, the power which propels it not yet aware" (427) ; and it is here that Hightower is forced to view all his past life, which, for the first time, he is able to see objectively. As the wheel slowly frees itself from the sand, Hightower gradually realizes that life cannot be lived in isolation, because the axle or spokes of the wheel cannot function if the rim is struck in sand. And with this realization, the "wheel whirls on. It is going fast and smooth now, because it is freed now of burden, of vehicle, axle, all" (430). In this passage, all of the divergent themes are brought together into full perspective as we see Hightower struggle with his inner self and finally attain complete self-realization of his place in the universe. Hightower's involvement, however, is forced upon him, but it is through this involvement that he attains knowledge of self. First, Byron involves him with Lena until finally it becomes his task to deliver Lena's child. And then, again through Byron's interference, the Lena-Joe connection is further correlated by Hightower's futile attempt to save Joe's life. Thus, through symbolic birth and death, Hightower becomes the connecting link which gives meaning both to himself and to Lena and Joe.

The circular image is first applied to Joe as a cage which keeps him imprisoned from mankind. The earliest instance of his im-

prisonment is seen in his life in the orphanage. Later in life, he
thinks of women, marriage, and children as additional ways to
keep men caged in. He even cuts off all buttons—again the
circular image—that women have sewed on his clothes. But the
strongest symbol of his imprisonment in a cage is expressed
through the conflicting white and black blood in his veins. Richard Chase connects linear images with Joe Christmas' life, even
though he then writes that Joe has "never escaped or broken"
from "the fateful circle."[6] Basically, the circular image is the
principal image with Joe as his life is presented in cyclic repeti-
tions: "From that night the thousand streets ran as one street,
with imperceptible corners and changes of scene, broken by intervals of begged and stolen rides, on trains and trucks, and on
country wagons . . . The street ran into Oklahoma and Missouri
and as far south as Mexico and then back north to Chicago and
Detroit and then back south again and at last to Mississippi"
(195).

Although Joe has spent his entire life trying to break out of
his circle, he finally realizes that he has lived only when he has
remained within the circle. Thus, he attains peace through self-
realization when he reaches an acceptance of his life. As he no
longer struggles with himself, he comes to the following recognition: ". . . during the last seven days he has had no paved street,
yet he has travelled farther than in all the thirty years before.
And yet he is still inside the circle. 'And yet I have been farther
in these seven days than in all the thirty years,' he thinks. 'But I
have never got outside that circle. I have never broken out of the
ring of what I have already done and cannot ever undo.' " (296).
Joe, in other words, comes finally to realize that his struggle of
thirty years was futile, since man can never escape from himself.
The acceptance of this fact gives him the first peace of mind that
he has ever had.

The circular image is used therefore to give additional meaning
to each character, to set up the sphere in which he acts, and to cor-
relate the action with the structure. Using the wheel image again,
Joanna Burden's house, and thus the cabin where Joe lives, serves
as the central locale of the novel. It is a place of birth and death
and is described as the axle of a wheel where the numerous paths

are "like wheelspokes" caused by "the Negro women who came
to the house from both directions up and down the road, following paths which had been years in the wearing and which radiated
from the house" (225). It is at the axle that Lena's child is born,
and when Hightower finally accepts his obligations to become
involved in the human race, he travels one of the many paths and
delivers Lena's child. This action becomes the symbolic connection between life and death which gives meaning to Hightower's
life. Structurally, then, Joe Christmas' actions are the central
ones of the novel and occupy the central portion of the novel,
while on all sides are the spokes of Hightower's actions finally
brought into contact with Joe through birth and death. And, as
mentioned above, the actions of Lena encompass the whole novel
as the rim encompasses the wheel.

Within the wheel stands the ever present community, and the
reaction of the various characters to the community offers a basic
approach to the novel. Phyllis Hirshleifer emphasizes isolation
of man in the novel,[7] while Cleanth Brooks sees in it man's relationship in the community.[8] These two views do not exclude
each other. The isolation of each character only reinforces his
struggle for status both with the community and with himself.
Light in August follows in the logical pattern set by Faulkner's
two earlier novels, *The Sound and the Fury* and *As I Lay Dying*.
The preceding novels dealt with man trying to find a meaningful
relationship with the immediate family, and this one deals with
man in relationship to the community and as an isolated being
unable to communicate with his fellow man.

Cleanth Brooks writes that the community serves as "the field
for man's actions and the norm by which his action is judged and
regulated."[9] But the difficulty here is that we do not have a sufficient picture of the norm. It would be accurate to regard the community as a force which man tries to assail or avoid. And as Miss
Hirshleifer writes: "The society through which Lena moves, the
people who give her food, lodging, money and transportation because of her patient understanding modesty are, after all, the
same people who crucify the Christmases whose evil arouses their
own."[10] It is, therefore, the responses of the community to the individual that become significant. While Lena evokes responses

for good, Joe Christmas seems to arouse their evil instincts, and Hightower arouses their suspicion. But these responses are not seen, as Brooks suggests, from the view of the community, but through the effects they produce on the individual character. Thus the community reacts in varying ways, but none of these reactions could accurately be considered as the norm of behavior. And even though Lena is able to evoke responses for good from various people, she remains outside the community. Each character in the novel is seen as a lonely individual pitted against some force either within or outside himself. Lena, Byron Bunch, Hightower, Christmas, Joanna Burden, Joe Brown, Doc Hines, and even people like Percy Grimm and McEachern stand outside the community. This is further emphasized by the fact that both Lena and Christmas are orphans who have no family whom they can return to. The community is also used as the objective commentator on the action. We get the long-range view usually from the point-of-view of the community, but nowhere during any of the long views does the community make any definite moral evaluations.[11]

The isolation theme is carried over into the structure of the novel. The novel may be broken down into many groups of seemingly isolated vignettes. Each scene, however, is part of one large thematic mosaic, and none could be successfully removed without destroying the whole. Likewise, each isolated character in each isolated scene is viewed in the final analysis as a part of the structure of a unified whole. Thus the isolation of each character is supported by the structural device of presenting the action of the novel in groups of vignettes.

II

Lena wills her own isolation. Although she could have left her uncle's home unmolested and by the front door, she chose to leave by the window which had played such a prominent part in her pregnancy. She never complains of her lot and never asks for help from anyone. However, she instinctively knows that people will help her; so she comes to accept their help at face value. Her simple faith in life is echoed by her belief that "a family ought to all be together when a chap comes. Specially the first one. I reckon the Lord will see to that" (18). Her responses to life are the simple and basic reactions founded on a simple philosophy of charity and hope. She is always anxious to help those people who give her assistance, and she would always "be obliged" if others would share her meager meals with her. She constantly feels the need to commune and share her experience with others. Even though she relies upon the kindness of strangers, her strength lies in the fact that she has assumed complete responsibility for her acts. She blames no person for her predicament, and she acknowledges no outside hostile force working against her. Lena, then, brings with her the potential salvation and redemption of Byron Bunch and Hightower by evoking from them responses for good and forcing them to become involved in responsibility.

Byron Bunch, during his seven years in Jefferson before Lena's arrival, had only one acquaintance, the Reverend Gail Hightower, who was an outcast completely isolated from the community. The community had never noticed Byron, except in a casual way to comment upon his idiosyncrasies, until he became involved with Lena. Merely by her passivity and her simple questions, Lena forces Byron to become involved. After revealing to her the identity of Joe Brown, Byron then feels responsible to her. This feeling of responsibility draws Byron out of his lethargic existence and forces him into the stream of life. He in turn tries to involve Hightower, who struggles against Byron's interference. Hightower has lived too long in his isolated world of self-abnegation and denial to see that Byron must feel responsible for Lena. He cannot understand Byron's actions and interprets them as possessing some ulterior motive. But Byron's actions are the outcome of more than thirty years of routine monotony and celibacy. Byron, like Lena, had willed his own isolation in Jefferson; however, with the appearance of Lena, he is forced to become involved in society. His potential redemption is that he is able to live outside himself and commune with another person; and even though this involvement was forced upon him, his strength and salvation lie in the fact that he willingly accepts the responsibility for his actions. Not only does he commit the necessary acts of preparing for Lena's child and acting as her protector, but also, he exceeds the demands made upon him when he follows after the fleeing Brown and confronts him even though he knows that he will be beaten. Thus Byron, after willing his own isolation, has involvement forced upon him which he willingly accepts.

Hightower's isolation is likewise somewhat self-imposed. Initially, the isolation derived from forces over which he had no control. His grandfather's ghost haunted his Calvinistic conscience until it forced him to marry a girl whom he did not love and subject her to his own ghosts. He is haunted by two conflicting views of his grandfather—that of the romantic cavalry officer galloping down the streets with drawn saber and that of the grandfather shot while stealing chickens, and furthermore, shot probably by some woman.[12] The seminary he attended acted not as a sanctuary from his phantoms, as he hoped it would, but rather as a means of furthering his ends and preparing him for a call to Jefferson. "God must call me to Jefferson because my life died there, was shot from the saddle of a galloping horse in a Jefferson street one night twenty years before it was ever born" (418). At the seminary, he met his future wife, who wanted to escape from the tedium of her life there. At Jefferson, he confused God with his grandfather, galloping horses with salvation, and the cavalry with Calvary. His sermons then reflected his own confusion and, as he later realizes, did not bring to the congregation the messages of hope and forgiveness. When his wife commits suicide as a result of Hightower's failure as a husband, the congregation then turns against Hightower. He then becomes the rejected and isolated minister. Therefore, part of his isolation is forced upon him, but in part it derives from his own inner failure to bring the past and present into a workable unity.[13]

Carl Benson writes: "Hightower shapes his own destiny by acts of will, and he is, therefore, morally accountable for his choice."[14] It seems, however, that Hightower's earlier life was shaped for him from forces of the past over which he had no control. These are the forces which ultimately cause him to be rejected by the Presbyterian congregation. It is only after his dismissal that Hightower wills his own destiny, and therefore becomes morally liable for it. His choice to stay in Jefferson despite persecution, disgrace, and physical violence results in his complete isolation. His moral responsibility derives from the sanctity of isolation away from the community. He thinks that because he suffered the disgrace and shame, the physical torment and pain, he has won the right to peace and solitude and the privilege of remaining un-involved in life. He refuses to accept responsibility for his past faults because his suffering has atoned for his previous errors—"*That's done now. That's past now. That's bought and paid for now.*" But with the entrance of Lena into Jefferson, Hightower is forcefully drawn into the stream of life again and realizes that the past has not been "bought and paid for now.". Hightower, therefore, cannot become the effective moral reflector of the novel until he is able to come to terms both with himself and with his fellow man, and until he assumes a place in society again and recognizes his responsibility to himself and his fellow man.

Lena, Byron, and Hightower all will their isolation. Joe Christmas' isolation is forced upon him early in his life by outside forces and attitudes. Part of his plight in life comes from the fact that he can never accept anything but partial responsibility for his acts and at the same time attempts to disclaim all responsibility for them. Just before killing Joanna, he thinks that "*Something is going to happen. Something is going to happen to me*" (106), which suggests that Christmas looks upon his violent actions as being compelled by exterior forces which relieve him of any personal responsibility. But then this only increases his predicament, because he *does* feel a partial responsibility for his actions. If, then, Christmas' life and attitudes are shaped by exterior forces, it is necessary, in order to understand his plight, to determine how much Christmas feels he should be held responsible for his acts.

Joe's earliest attitudes were formulated in the orphanage. It was here that he first discovered that he possessed Negro blood—a fact that in one way or another controlled or affected his every act throughout life. His remaining life was spent trying to bring these two irreconcilable opposites into a significant relationship. His unknown father bequeathed him his Negro blood, "not only the blood of slaves but even a little of the very blood which had enslaved it; himself his own battleground, the scene of his own vanquishment and the mausoleum of his defeat."[15] His heritage, over which he had no control, is the strongest influence upon his life. At the orphange he is first called "nigger." The blood cages him in, and the vigilance of old Doc Hines sets him apart from the rest of the orphans. He is unable to establish a meaningful relationship with any of the other children, and he senses his difference.

One experience at the orphanage, especially, has multiple consequences for Christmas. When he is discovered stealing the dietician's toothpaste, he expects punishment and instead is bribed with more money than he knew existed. This experience becomes the determining factor in his attitude toward the order of existence, women, and sex throughout the rest of his life. Since he was kept in suspense for several days desiring punishment which never came, he was left confused as to the meaning of his act. Therefore, during the rest of his life when the pattern or order of existence is broken, the result is usually disastrous. When he transgresses McEachern's rules he expects and receives punishment, which accords with his idea of the order of things. This is again why he detests the interference of Mrs. McEachern. She, like the dietician, represents a threat to the settled order of human existence. Or else, with each prostitute during his years on the road, he would tell her that he was a Negro, which always brought one reaction. When this pattern is broken by the prostitute who did not care whether he was Negro or not, his reactions are violent:

> "What about it? You look all right. You ought to seen the shine I turned out just before your turn came." She was looking at him. She was quite still now. "Say, what do you think this dump is, anyhow? The Ritz hotel?" Then she quit talking. She was watching his face and she began to move backward slowly before him, staring at him, her face draining, her mouth open to scream. Then she did scream. It took two policemen to subdue him. At first they thought that the woman was dead.
>
> He was sick after that. He did not know until then that there were white women who would take a man with a black skin. He stayed sick two years.

Thus his violent outburst comes from the unconscious desire to punish the dietician who had first violated his pattern of order. The same reaction is seen in his relationship with Joanna Burden. For three years, their relationship conformed to an ordered (though unorthodox) pattern; but when Joanna broke this pattern with her demands that Christmas take over her finances, go to a Negro school, and finally that he pray with her in order to be saved, he again reacted violently to this violation of his concept of an ordered existence.

His basic hatred for women ultimately returns to this episode. The dietician in violating his order of existence also attempted to destroy his individuality. Thus the effeminizing efforts of Mrs. McEachern to soften his relations with his foster father are rejected because if he yielded to them, he would face the possibility of losing the firm and ordered relation with McEachern. As long as he maintains this masculine relationship with McEachern, he feels that he retains his individuality.

And, finally, the childhood episode with the dietician is reflected in his sex life. The toothpaste becomes the basic symbol. At the same time that it is a cleansing agent, it also serves as a phallic symbol. The result of the scene is his utter sickness caused by the "pinkwomansmelling obscurity behind the curtain" and the "listening to his insides, waiting with astonished fatalism for what was about to happen to him" (107). Each subsequent sex relation, therefore, brings a gilt feeling to Christmas. He associated sex with filth, sickness, violation of order, and the potential loss of individuality. Likewise, it is significant that each of his subsequent encounters with sex is accompanied by strong sensory images. When he beats the young Negro girl, it is amid the strong odors of the barn. Again he is reminded of the sickness caused by the toothpaste: "There was something in him trying to get out, like when he had used to think of toothpaste. But he could not move at once, standing there smelling the woman, smelling the Negro all at once" (137). And later his first encounter with Bobbie Allen is in the restaurant where he goes to order food, and finally, he meets Joanna in her kitchen when he is stealing food from her. Each of these sensory occurrences recalls to him the scene with the dietician and again threatens the loss of individuality and the breaking of an ordered existence.

Christmas' need for order is violated in turn by each of the women with whom he comes into contact. The lesson he learned early in life was that "he and the man could always count upon one another, depend upon one another; that it was the woman alone who was unpredictable." It was the woman who always broke the pattern of order. First the dietician, then Mrs. McEachern violated his concept of order, and then Bobbie Allen turned violently against him at the time when he most needed her. The last woman to break his order of existence was Joanna Burden, who paid for it with her life. The women, then, serve as the destroyers of order. This is brought out mechanically by Faulkner by using the Biblical concept of woman as being unclean. Their menstrual period breaks the order of their life and then comes to represent their unordered and unclean life. They are the "smooth and superior shape in which volition dwelled doomed to be at stated and inescapable intervals victims of periodical filth" (161). The first time he learned of their monthly occurrences, his reactions were violent and ended in a blood baptism—the blood being taken from a young sheep that he killed. But even then he rejected this knowledge so that when Bobbie Allen tried to explain the same thing to him, again his reactions were violent, this time ending with his vomiting. When he next sees Bobbie, he takes her with force and animal brutality. Again, he seems to be reacting against his initial introduction to sex through the dietician, again asserting his masculinity by forcing order upon the woman.

Christmas' great need for order reverts basically to the two bloods in him which are in constant conflict. As stated previously, his blood is his own battleground. He can neither accept nor reject his mixture of blood, and neither can he bring these two elements into a workable solution. Christmas' plight results from his inability to secure a suitable position in society: "Sometimes he would remember how he had once tricked or teased white men into calling him a Negro in order to fight them, to beat them or be beaten; now he fought the Negro who called him white. He was in the north now, in Chicago and then Detroit. He lived with

Negroes, shunning white people. He ate with them, slept with them, belligerent, unpredictable, uncommunicative" (196-197). He searched for a society that could accept both elements of his blood and, unable to find this, he isolates himself from human society.

Christmas' youthful love for Bobbie Allen existed on an idealistic plane because he was able to confess his Negro blood to her and be accepted by her as an individual. However, her betrayal of his love accompanied by her taunts of "nigger bastard" and "clod-hopper" implants the idea in his mind that due to his blood he must remain the isolated being.

His search for peace, then, is a search for someone who could accept Joe Christmas as an individual despite his conflicting blood. When Joanna Burden asks Christmas how he knows he has Negro blood, he responds: "I don't know it. . . . If I'm not, damned if I haven't wasted a lot of time" (223). He has spent his whole life and energy trying to reconcile these two bloods, and if he has no Negro blood then all the efforts of his life have been to no avail.[56]

Joanna Burden should have been the person who could have accepted Joe for what he was. By the time of their involvement, Christmas no longer seems to revolt against being called a Negro. But Joanna fails him. In being corrupted by him, she seems to enjoy the corruption even more by screaming "nigger, nigger" as he makes love to her. At thirty and thirty-three, Joe has learned to accept this name-calling without the accompanying violent reactions; he is living in partial peace with himself, even though this peace had been found only in complete isolation. He must reject all of mankind in order to find peace. This is seen when Byron offers Christmas food and the offer is rejected with the cursory statement: "Keep your muck." Therefore, when Joanna offers him jobs, wants him to go to school, or tries to get him to pray, he feels that she is trying to destroy his isolation and peace. He is then forced to kill her or allow his own individuality, order, and peace to be destroyed by her. Faulkner conveys this on the story level simply by the fact that Joanna planned to kill Christmas and would have succeeded if the pistol had not failed her. Christmas is then forced to kill her in self-protection. His life, his individuality, his peace, and his order would have been destroyed by Joanna had he yielded to her. And her death is accompanied by Christmas' refrain: *"all I wanted was peace."* But even at Joanna Burden's house, Joe could not attain his desired peace with himself because the warring elements of his blood compelled him to tell others that he was a Negro. At least, he confessed to Joanna and Brown. If, then, he could achieve peace only by isolating himself from people and by rejecting all responsibliity toward society, he could never attain inner peace until he could accept himself and his own blood, both Negro and white.

Since Joanna was an overpowering threat to Joe's sense of peace and order, he realized that he must murder her or be destroyed by her. But the murder was not one in cold blood. There are elaborate and symbolic rituals preceding the actual performance. First comes the realization that he has been tricked and fooled by Joanna, that she lied to him about her age, and that she is destroying his peace. He then symbolically liberates himself from all women as he cuts the buttons off his clothes "with the cold and bloodless deliberation of a surgeon" (193) severing the umbilical cord. Completely naked, he undergoes a cleansing and baptismal ritual as he walks through the wet dew and the tall "thighdeep grass." "He stood with his hands on his hips, naked, thighdeep in the dusty weeds, while the car came over the hill and approached, the lights full upon him. He watched his body grow white out of the darkness like a kodak print emerging from the liquid" (94). The interplay of the darkness on his white body and of the car light penetrating the darkness and illuminating his whiteness against a black background suggests the conflicting elements of his blood. After revealing his nudity to the passing car, he goes to the barn to sleep for the night because he wants to be near the smell of horses. Thus the use of the "thighdeep dusty weeds" as a phallic symbol and his desire to be near the man-smell of horses again support his basic need to deny and to reject the effeminate and woman world.[17] Following a brief sleep, he becomes immersed in phallic images—the ladder, grass, lumber, icicles, and his own dark serge trousers set off by his white shirt. The cracked mirror in the cabin reflects Joe's conflict as he can see and come to terms with only half of his self. In the "small valley in which a spring rose," he rests and goes through another cleansing episode as he shaves, this time using the water from the spring as the mirror, thereby severing connections with all man-made objects. His next act is to destroy the whiskey which had been his chief means of income in the Jefferson society.

His last act before the murder is to visit two sections of town. He goes first to the white section, which he rejects because he senses his isolation from it. He then goes to the Negro section, where he is rejected and where he realizes that his isolation is complete, utter, and irrevocable. He then makes his way back to the house where the murder is to take place.

The entire scene (89-106) is interspersed with numerous images of black and white; and through it all, Christmas carries his razor, which he is tempted to use, not in the white section he rejected, but in the Negro section where he is rejected. And as a thematic refrain, the phrase *"All I wanted was peace"* runs through the whole scene.

Thus, Joe's elaborate preparations for the murder and finally the act itself sever him forever from any hope of becoming a meaningful part of society.

It is significant that he does not attempt to escape. He never leaves the vicinity of the crime. On the Tuesday after the Friday of the crime, he enters the Negro church and curses God. This is the height of his conflict.[18] The white blood can no longer remain pacified and must express itself in violence. It remains now for Joe to come to terms with the conflicting elements within himself, and this can be done only within the circle of his own self; consequently, there is no need for Joe to leave the immediate neighborhood of his crime.

When Joe exchanges his shoes for the Negro woman's brogans, he seems to accept his heritage for the first time in his life: "It seemed to him that he could see himself being hunted by white men at last into the black abyss which had been waiting, trying, for thirty years to drown him and into which now and at last he had actually entered, bearing now upon his ankles the definite and ineradicable gauge of its upward moving" (289). And with his acceptance of his black blood, Joe Christmas finds peace for the first time in his life. Like Lena Grove, who always accepted her responsibility, Joe realizes now that in order to find peace, he must accept full responsibility for his heritage and actions. And again like Lena, when he accepts this responsibility, he finds peace and contentment, and he becomes unified with nature: "The air, inbreathed, is like spring water. He breathes deep and slow, feeling with each breath himself diffuse in the neutral grayness, becoming one with loneliness and quiet that has never known fury or despair. That was all I wanted, he thinks, in a quiet and slow amazement. That was all, for thirty years. That didn't seem to be a whole lot to ask in thirty years" (289). Following this recognition and acceptance, he undergoes once more a symbolic cleansing ritual. This time using the Negro's shoes to sharpen his razor, Christmas prepares himself for his return to town in order to assume responsibility for his actions. It is when Joe accepts his Negro heritage and recognizes that he can never escape from himself that he breathes quietly for the first time in his life. "Then one day he was no longer hungry. It came sudden and peaceful" (292). This sudden recognition that he is no longer hungry becomes significant against the background of Joe's earlier life, which was filled with a constant struggle against hunger. That is, when he accepts himself, he symbolically becomes at peace with his tormenting hunger and also he sleeps peacefully for the first time.

With his acceptance of his responsibility and his recognition of his heritage, Joe can once more approach others. This is revealed by the scenes which immediately precede and follow Joe's self-realization. In the first scene, Joe approaches a Negro in order to ask him the day of the week, and his mere appearance creates astonishment and terror in the Negro's mind. He flees from Christmas in utter horror. But immediately after Joe has come to peace with himself, he approaches another Negro who quite naturally and nonchalantly offers him a ride to Mottstown. Joe now has achieved an acceptance for himself: " 'Now I can let go for a while,' he thinks. 'I haven't let go for seven days, so I guess I'll let go for a while.' He thinks that perhaps, sitting, with the wagon's motion to lull him, he will sleep. But he does not sleep. He is not sleepy or hungry or even tired. He is somewhere between and among them, suspended, swaying to the motion of the wagon without thought, without feeling. He has lost account of time, distance . . ." (296). Thus Joe has traveled farther in the last seven days than in all the years of his life, because for the first time he has come to a complete recognition of his own life and sees that the true value or meaning of life is within his circle where he is able to achieve an understanding with himself.

Joe's plight in life, however, is not resolved. He could gain a partial truce with society by isolating himself from this society; or else, he could attain a full acceptance of himself, but note that this was achieved while outside the community in complete isolation. Once he has recognized his responsibility, he must then return to the community. And once again in the community, he comes to the realization that he can never be accepted by society. The realization of his complete rejection is made more terrible by the wild rantings of his own grandfather, who demands his death.[19] Thus, if old Doc Hines must persecute his own grandson, Joe realizes that there can be peace for him only in death. His escape finally, however, seems to be not so much because of the fanaticism of Old Doc Hines, but rather because of the quiet persuasion of Mrs. Hines. Her appearance at the jail was probably Joe's final proof of the woman's need to destroy his individuality. Doc and Mrs. Hines then contribute to Joe's death since they set peaceful elements into contention again. Consequently, his escape is an escape from woman and also a search for peace and order through death. It is, therefore, logical that after his escape he runs first to a Negro cabin and then to Hightower's house. Through Mrs. Hines, Hightower has become the symbol of hope and peace to Christmas, and in his search for peace through death, he chooses Hightower's house as his sanctuary in which he passively accepts his crucifixion. His failure to fire the pistol is symbolic of his acceptance of his crucifixion and death and of his recognition that he can find peace only in death.

The violent death and castration of Christmas at the hands of Percy Grimm implant in our memories the atrocities that man is capable of committing against his fellow man. Grimm becomes the extreme potential of all the community when society refuses to accept its responsibility to mankind. Or as Hightower uttered when he first heard about Christmas: "Poor man. Poor mankind." That is, Joe's death is not as much a tragedy for Joe as it is a tragedy for the society which would allow such a crime as Grimm's to be perpetrated. In Grimm's act, therefore, we see the failure of man to attain recognition, sympathy, or communion among other men and society's failure to accept man in the abstract.

But Joe's death was not in vain. Through his death and through the birth of Lena's child, Hightower has attained salvation in life by arriving at a complete realization of his own responsibility. Earlier in life, Hightower thought that through suffering he had won for himself the privilege of remaining un-involved in life. " 'Because all that any man can hope for is to be permitted to live quietly among his fellows' " (64). But with the appearance of Lena, he becomes once more drawn into the active stream of life. This participation was not voluntary but forced upon him in the first instance (delivering Lena's child), but after rejecting Mrs. Hines's pleas, his second act (attempting to save Joe's life) is entirely voluntary. Originally the attraction of Hightower and Byron to each other depended upon both being isolated from the community; but as Byron becomes involved, he draws Hightower in also. Until after Lena gives birth, Hightower struggles to retain his isolation and advises Byron to do the same: "Go away, Byron. Go Away. Now. At once. Leave this place forever, this terrible place, this terrible place, this terrible place" (25). But Byron's involvement is too deep. Hightower's struggle for isolation becomes more intense as he sees himself threatened with involvement: " 'But it is not right to bother me, to worry me, when I have—when I have taught myself to stay—have been taught by them to stay—That this should come to me taking me after I am old, and reconciled to what they deemed—' Once before Byron saw him sit while sweat ran down his face like tears; now he sees the tears themselves run down the flabby cheeks like sweat" (319). He is then asked by Byron and Mrs. Hines to lie for Joe Christmas' (and in Hightower's words, mankind's) benefit. His refusal is his last futile but passionate effort to retain his isolation:

"It's not because I cant, dont dare to," he says: "it's because I wont! I wont! do you hear?" He raises his hands from the chair arms. "It's because I wont do it!" Byron watches the other, thinking *It aint me he is shouting at. It's like he knows there is something nearer him than me to convince of that.* Because now Hightower is shouting, "I wont do it! I wont!" with his hands raised and clenched, his face sweating, his lip lifted upon his clenched and rotting teeth from about which the long sagging of flabby and putty colored flesh falls away. Suddenly his voice rises higher yet. "Get out!" he screams. "Get out of my house! Get out of my house!" (342).

His refusal, of course, is not a refusal to utter the lie but a refusal to become an active participant in the community and thus become involved in responsibility again.

But Hightower goes to the cabin and successfully delivers Lena's child.[20] This act of giving life to Lena's child becomes symbolic of Hightower's restoration to life. Immediately after the act, he walks back to town thinking that he won't be able to sleep, but he does sleep as peacefully as Lena's newborn child. He notices for the first time the peaceful serenity of the August morning, "The intermittent sun, the heat. The savage and fecund odor of the earth, the woods, the loud silence" (356). He becomes immersed in the miracle of life and realizes that "life comes to the old man yet" (355). He views the birth as a sign of good fortune and an omen of good will. Therefore, this act of involvement and responsibility has restored Hightower to the human race. This was Monday morning. Monday afternoon, Hightower is faced with his second act of involvement when Christmas flees to his house for sanctuary. This violence which Hightower must face is his payment for recognizing his responsibility in life. But having assisted in the birth of Lena's child and having recognized his involvement in life, he can no longer retract. Therefore, having acknowledged a partial responsibility, he must now perform his act of complete involvement in life by attempting to assume responsibility for Joe Christmas. "Listen to me. He was here that night. He was with me the night of the murder. I swear to God" (406). And even though Hightower fails Christmas, he has achieved salvation for himself. He does not realize this until later on in the evening when the whole meaning of his life evolves in front of him "with the slow implacability of a mediaeval torture instrument." And through this wheel image, he sees that man cannot isolate himself from the faces surrounding the wheel. Man must become a part of the community and must assume responsibility not only for his own actions but also for the actions of his fellow man.

Through symbolic life and death, Hightower has found peace in life, and the principal correlation between Lena and Joe assumes further significance. They first met by the column of smoke which announced Lena's arrival and Joe's departure. And the contrast between these two opposing entities carries throughout the novel. Malcolm Cowley's objection that the themes "have little relation to each other," or Irwin Howe's reservations concerning the "troublesome problems of organization" and the "evident flaw" of "looseness" seem unwarranted.[21] The images of the curve and circle are used in connection with both. With Lena these images imply an acceptance and unity with life, but with Joe they represent the society from which he is isolated and the cage in which he lives. Joe had been in Jefferson for three years when Lena arrived at the end of this third year. However, she comes to terms with the town almost overnight, while Joe was never able to adjust himself. This is the result of basic differences in their character: Lena is talkative, Joe reticent; Lena is willing to share her food, Joe rejects all proffered food; Lena's isolation is self-imposed, Joe's isolation is imposed upon him; Lena is in a search of life, Joe is in flight from life; Lena never complains of life, Joe is in constant conflict with life; Lena brings life and affirmation to the community, Joe brings death and rejection to himself and the community; and finally, Lena finds her peace in life while Joe can find peace only in death. Thus Joe and Lena can never encounter each other because they are almost diametrically opposed. But still, they bring about the resolution by performing their acts and involvement on the same ground. Again the circle of smoke first introduces them to each other. Then we find that Lena's lover is Christmas' partner. They are connected through Brown, who has lived with both, betrayed both, and caused both to "take to the road." Lena goes to Christmas' cabin, the scene of Joanna's brutal death, to give birth and renewal to life. It is here that Hightower goes directly from the birth of

Lena's son to Joe's death. And, finally, Christmas' grandparents assist in giving birth to Lena's child, which Mrs. Hines confuses with Milly's child. " 'It's Joey . . .it's my Milly's little boy.' " This results ultimately in confusing Lena as to the paternity of her child: " 'She keeps on talking about him like his pa was that . . . the one in jail, that Mr. Christmas. She keeps on, and then I get mixed up and it's like sometimes I cant—like I am mixed up too and I think that his pa is that Mr.—Mr. Christmas too—' " (359). Thus through life and death, Lena and Joe are symbolically joined together. Life is reaffirmed for mankind through the birth of Lena's child, the death of Joe Christmas, and the resurrection of Hightower. The child then becomes the symbol of the future world which brings all people together, giving new life and hope to all.

This redemption could only be achieved through the death of Joe Christmas, which suggests finally why Christmas has been consistently described in Christian imagery and symbolism.[22] The use of the Christian myth in connection with Joe does not necessarily imply that Joe should be considered a Christ figure.[23] But rather, by using the Christ story as a point of reference or an analogy, Joe's temptation, his struggle, his search for the meaning of life, his persecution, and his death become more meaningful, and each scene becomes more intense merely by the comparison. Numerous parallels connect Christmas' life to that of Christ, but the myth, if used, should be applied only in its broadest connotations. As stated previously, the analogy in any specific scene serves to intensify Joe's dilemma. For example, in the scene of the Sunday Catechism lesson by McEachern, Joe's resistance to his adopted father takes on a deeper meaning when it is compared with the temptation and suffering which Christ underwent rather than adopt a religion foreign to his mission. Again, when Joanna Burden tries to tempt him from his accepted way of life, the temptation becomes more intensely significant when viewed in the light of Christ's temptation. Therefore, Joe's whole life and his struggles can be universalized by correlating them with the life of Christ.

In conclusion, Faulkner views pessimistically the struggle of Christmas to gain recognition in the world. Because of the mixture of his blood, he can never be wholly accepted by either the white or the Negro. His plight is that of a man lost between two worlds where he can find acceptance in neither. His mixed blood denies to him any hope of community with his fellow man. Knowing this, Christmas cannot come to any terms either with society or with himself. Like Christ, he figures the stranger in a hostile and alien universe. But Faulkner does seem to offer some hope through the birth of Lena's child, and through Lena's affirmation in life. However, Lena serves basically the same thematic function as Dilsey in *The Sound and the Fury*, that is, a substructure of the novel through which the tragedy of the central character becomes more pertinent. But Hightower adds a further level, and through his moral reclamation we view man recognizing his responsibility to both himself and to his fellow man.

The Heart Is a Lonely Hunter:
A Southern Waste Land

by
Horace Taylor

ALTHOUGH PRAISED QUITE lavishly at its publication and apparently still quite highly regarded by critics, Carson McCullers' *The Heart Is a Lonely Hunter* has suffered the curious fate in recent years of attracting little or no critical attention.[1] This is an undeserved fate.

The novel deals poignantly with a characteristically modern literary theme: the spiritual isolation and loneliness of man. In a series of sharply observed character studies, the author reveals the horrible spiritual isolation that is the lot of five people existing in a stagnant Southern town:[2] Mick, an imaginative young girl entering her teens; Biff, a tavern proprietor with a penchant for freaks and the downtrodden; Jake, a frustrated Marxian labor agitator; Dr. Copeland, a disillusioned champion of the rights of the Negro; and Singer, a deaf mute, who is all things to the other four.

Singer is the catalyst in the interlocking lives of these four people. He appears to supply something to each of these lonely people that is lacking in their social intercourse with all others. It is not that Singer supplies some active ingredient in these relationships that causes Mick, Biff, Dr. Copeland, and Jake to seek his company so avidly, but that Singer is "sort of a home-made God" to each of them. It is precisely because Singer is a deaf mute and a patient, considerate man that each of the four is drawn to him. Thus, they can make of him what they will. To Dr. Copeland, a frustrated Negro crusader for the betterment of his race, Singer is the only white man whom he likes, simply because Singer lacks the usual contemptuous arrogance of the white southerner. Dr. Copeland can unburden his pent-up heart to Singer, something he can do with no other person, Negro or white. Similarly, Singer serves somewhat the same function with Jake, the near-insane labor agitator. Singer is the only man besides Biff who does not ridicule Jake when he is on one of his frequent hysterical talking binges. For Mick, a sensitive, highly imaginative, twelve-year-old girl, Singer's role is somewhat more complex: he serves as a kind of repository for her secret aspirations.

Of the four people, Biff is the least affected by the illusion of Singer. Biff is the curious student and spectator of human relationships, and observes with keen interest the curiously intricate relationship that Singer has with the others. Yet, Biff too is caught up in the spell of Singer, though more from curiosity than from need, and goes up to Singer's room almost as often as do the other three. Thus we can see at the outset something of the bond that exists between Singer and the other major characters.

But what kind of a man is Singer and what does he possess to inspire such attachment? The answer—literally nothing. Singer is an illusion: hence the epithet cast at him by Biff of "a home-made God," that each of the characters creates to satisfy his own desperate emotional needs. Unknown to them, Singer is as empty and as fearful as they, but because he is a mute and unable to express his equally terrible needs, they never recognize his loneliness. Moreover, Singer also has an emotional symbol which he clings to, his mute moronic friend, Antonapoulos.

The relationship that exists between Antonapoulos and Singer is significant since it forms one of the basic links in the action of *The Heart Is a Lonely Hunter*. Singer can only be what he is to the others because Antonapoulos bears a like relationship to Singer, or he thinks that Antonapoulos does. In this relationship Antonapoulos gives almost nothing and Singer almost all. Antonapoulos, a complete endomorph and a moron in addition, takes all of Singer's largesse and gives only a passive silence in return. But Singer is content with this state of affairs: he can express himself to Antonapoulos without restraint, even though it is highly likely that Singer's eloquent hand-talk is ignored by Antonapoulos. For Singer, Antonapoulos is the perfect conversationalist: he says nothing, thus allowing Singer to express himself to his heart's content in much the same way that Singer allows his talking friends to speak to him without reply. When Antonapoulos is placed in an insane asylum by his cousin for degeneracy, Singer is greatly dejected, but consoles himself in the knowledge that he can pay his friend occasional visits in the asylum. This is the situation as it stands between Singer and Antonapoulos when Singer's relationship with the other four characters forms. The novel is thus a study of what happens to Singer, Antonapoulos, Biff, Mick, Dr. Copeland, Jake, and several minor characters in the course of a year. Presumably the action begins when Antonapoulos is already in the asylum and ends shortly after the suicide of Singer.

It is evident at the outset that a deep-rooted narcissistic quality exists in all of these people, a degenerate sensibility that needs a human mirror in the form of a passive listener to reflect itself against. They do not want an active friend to reciprocate their needs, since that would involve a give-and-take relationship. Each of them is almost completely wrapped up in the tremendous urgency of the expression of his own desires and is almost completely oblivious to both the needs and character of the others. The only one with a reasonable amount of spiritual insight is Biff, and in him this stems more from curiosity than from actual sympathy.

The spiritual blindness of Jake, Dr. Copeland, and Mick, particularly the first two, can be seen in two incidents. In the first of these, by a pure coincidence all four dependents arrive at Singer's room at the same time. The initial result is strained silence: "Singer was bewildered. Always each of them had so much to say. Yet now that they were together they were silent. When they came in he had expected an outburst of some kind. In a vague way he had expected this to be the end of something. But in the room there was only a feeling of strain." They cannot say anything. Each of them regards the others as intruders and considers his own need of Singer paramount. When they finally are able to talk it is about the most superficial subject of all, the weather, and even then "each person addressed his words mainly to the mute. Their thoughts seemed to converge in him as the spokes of a wheel lead to the central hub." But this strained silence does not last long: "They discussed the weather some more. Each one seemed to be waiting for the others to go. Then on an impulse they all rose to leave at the same time."

What is revealed in the incident is the unconscious but utter selfishness of these people. Each of them is solely concerned with the pouring out of his own inner compulsions to Singer. The ultimate in selfishness is revealed by the fact that it never occurs to any of them that Singer could serve the same function to each of them.

Singer vaguely recognizes the complexity of the situation, but its psychological impact escapes him. In a letter to Antonapoulos he confesses his bewilderment on the score of his friends:

> They are all very busy people. . . . I do not mean that they work at their jobs all day and night but that they have much business in their minds always that will not let them rest. They come up to my room and talk to me until I do not understand how a person can open and shut his or her mouth so much without being weary. (However the New York Cafe owner is different . . . he watches. The others all have something they love more than eating or sleeping or wine or friendly company. That is why they are always busy.)
>
> That is the way they talk when they come to my room. Those words in their hearts do not let them rest so they are always very busy. . . . They all came to my room at the same time today. They sat like they were from different cities. They were even rude. . . .

Thus, Singer summarizes what went on in the meeting and recognizes the terrible need of his friends to talk. Though he recognizes their need of expression, he is scarcely conscious of his own need— that Antonapoulos serves precisely the same function for him.

But let us hold our analysis in abeyance until we look at the second incident, which forms a kind of sequel to the first. It is an attempt made by Jake and Dr. Copeland to combine forces to actualize their idealism. But the meeting is disastrous from the start. Dr. Copeland is too conscious of Jake's being the hated white man, and both of them are too obsessed with their fixed ideas to compromise at all with each other. Jake sees the basic problem of society as that of labor exploitation, while Dr. Copeland sees it as that of the down-trodden Negro, and never the twain shall meet. The interview thus ends in mutual curses and recriminations. Both men are frustrated idealists who cling to their visions with all the crazed fanaticism of those who are driven to the brink of insane despair by ridicule and indifference. Jake and Dr. Copeland appear to build their very existence around their idealism; they are consumed by the need of vindication of their ideas.

Now we are ready to resume our analysis. Each of these people is a kind of universe unto himself, but incomplete to the extent that he needs another person to express himself to, a mirror to reflect against. These people reflect keenly the disintegration of a way of life.

The society in which they live has lost its communal spirit and is composed of but an indeterminate number of individuals living in psychological isolation from each other. Even those who would normally bear the closest of relations—husband and wife, father and children—are psychological strangers. Alice, married to Biff for ten years, is essentially a stranger to him, as are Dr. Copeland's children to him. Biff's reactions to Alice may be taken as typical:

> He was sorry he had talked to Alice. With her, silence was better. Being around that woman always made him different from his real self. It made him tough and small and common as she was. . . .
>
> Alice was almost asleep again, and through the mirror he watched her with detachment. There was no distinctive point about her on which he could fasten his attention, and his gaze glided from her pale brown hair to the stumpy outline of her feet beneath the cover. . . . When he was away from her there was no one feature that stood out in his mind and he remembered her as a complete unbroken figure.

Biff knows little about Alice and doesn't care to know much. She is a nonentity as far as he is concerned, even though she is his wife. The only bond they share is that of custom. They have lived together for ten years, after which it is easier to maintain the status quo than to separate. Biff and Alice truly represent a death in life, going through the empty ritual of a marriage without affection. Thus it is not surprising that when Alice suddenly dies, Biff is not heartbroken. In fact, he seems to feel a sense of relief at being a widower.

Similarly, Dr. Copeland's children are strangers to him. Between Dr. Copeland and his daughter, Portia, there is at best an armed truce. She visits him only out of a sense of filial piety.

Through Biff and Alice, Dr. Copeland and his children, Carson McCullers draws a poignant picture of a Southern Waste Land. These people are spiritually dead for the most part, having lost almost completely the bond of communal spirituality with their fellow men. They go through a prescribed but too often empty ritual of friendship and love, doing whatever custom calls for without any sense of sharing feeling. They are the hollow men of a society that is spiritually dead.

In such a society there are but two ways for its members to express themselves: they must make a violent, generally antisocial assertion of the individual ego, as Jake does; or remain inert and follow unthinkingly an empty ritual of routine existence, as do the majority. Only the sensitive, those filled with an oppressive sense of personal disquiet and psychological claustrophobia rebel against society. But it is significant to note that they know not what they are rebelling against; they know only that the welling up forces in them need—demand—an outlet. When the normative bonds of a society die, its sensitive individuals are left in spiritual isolation and they are denied social release. Thus, when the communal spirit that forms the psychological basis of a society is gone, its members can either die spiritually with it or flap about frantically like fish out of water, as do Jake, Dr. Copeland, Mick, and Singer.

Jake and Dr. Copeland never once suspect that their passionate championing of economic and social justice is but a pyschological revolt against the death clasp of society. They are excellent illustrations of why social crusaders so often fail. One cannot correct the abuses of a society by agitation for social reform when that society is dead or dying. Thus, the Jakes and the Dr. Copelands are always frustrated in their railing against social and economic abuses. Reform is a shortsighted expedient, since it deals at best only with the more superficial layers of the social organism and does not penetrate to its psychological core. Moreover, the causes that Jake and Dr. Copeland champion are in essence pretexts—psychological "whipping boys," convenient evils to let off steam against. Like most utopians they cannot realize that social abuses cannot be eradicated by improving the physical state of man.

Ultimately, the problem of both the society and its individuals is a religious one. The society has no substratum of faith to give its individuals a sense of belonging. Never once in the actions of the major characters in *The Heart Is a Lonely Hunter* is religion referred to in a meaningful way. Ironically, this lack of religious impulses becomes even more striking when one realizes that this town lies in the middle of the "Bible-belt." Dr. Copeland summarily dismisses the faith of his children as childish ignorance. Then, too, at the time when Biff would most need the consolation of religion—at the death of his wife—there is no mention of it, though he bears some of the external trappings such as the widower's black arm band. The society of Biff, Dr. Copeland, Singer, Mick, and Jake is a secular one and they have become "atomized," that is, their society has become a loose aggregate of individuals bearing little or no intrinsic relation to each other. The psycho-religious bond of community has been lost and only the empty forms of communal existence remain. These people for all their social, religious, or political ties are no better than strangers to each other.

The society portrayed in the novel exists in a kind of limbo of static death, of "death in life." Despite the violence, despite all of the desperate urgency of the sensitive people—nothing happens. Each of these people—Mick, Jake, Dr. Copeland, Singer, and Biff—is a solipsist, completely bound up within himself. The recognition of his essential psycho-spiritual isolation drives Singer to suicide. The others are perhaps protected from the horrifying realization of their condition by the curious self-sufficiency of their causes and needs. While there was probably no direct influence of T. S. Eliot upon Carson McCullers, it is interesting to observe that the same controlling concept that we find in *The Waste Land* adapts itself to the art of this important novel.

Notes

DONALD E. STANFORD

[1]*The Letter-Book of Samuel Sewall,* in *Collections of the Massachusetts Historical Society,* sixth series (1886-1888), II, 274.

[2]*The Poetical Works of Edward Taylor* (New York, 1939). An enlarged edition of Taylor's poems edited by Donald E. Stanford is scheduled to be published by the Yale University Press, Spring, 1960.

[3]*The Oxford Anthology of American Literature* (New York, 1938), pp. 60-63.

[4]Norman Grabo has prepared an edition of the sermons as his doctoral dissertation at the University of California at Los Angeles. This article was written before Grabo completed his dissertation, which I have not seen.

[5]"CHRISTOGRAPHIA, or A Discourse toching Christs Person, Natures, the Personall Union of the Natures. Qualifications, and Operations Opened, Confirmed, and Practically improoved in severall sermons delivered upon Certain Sacrament Dayes unto the Church and the people of God in Westfield." A note on the title page states that this was a volume of fifteen sermons. It now contains only fourteen sermons with the original Sermon 14 missing.

[6]The sermon is reprinted in part in Perry Miller and Thomas H. Johnson, *The Puritans* (New York, 1938), pp. 350-367.

[7]*The Works of that Famous and Worthy Minister of Christ* (London, 1631), II, 673, as quoted in W. Fraser Mitchell, *English Pulpit Oratory from Andrewes to Tillotson* (London, 1932), pp. 99-100.

[8]Mitchell, *English Pulpit Oratory,* p. 114.

[9]*The Intellectual Life of Colonial New England* (New York, 1956), p. 157.

[10]On the orthodox Calvinistic conception of the Lord's Supper expressed in Taylor's *Sacramental Meditations,* see Donald E. Stanford, "Edward Taylor and the Lord's Supper," *AL,* XXVII (1955), 172-178; Donald E. Stanford, "Sacramental Meditations by Edward Taylor," *YULG,* XXXI (1956), 61-75. On Taylor's Calvinistic sense of sin, see Donald E. Stanford, "Nineteen Unpublished Poems by Edward Taylor," *AL,* XXIX (1957), 18-46.

[11]"The Westminster Confession is a classic of Calvinism," writes John T. McNeill, *The History and Character of Calvinism* (New York, 1954), p. 325.

[12]*The Puritan Pronaos* (New York, 1936), p. 10.

161

[13]*The Intellectual Life of Colonial New England* (New York, 1956), p. 11. He also states (p. 160) that Jonathan Edwards was the first New England Calvinist. In his biographical sketch of Taylor, Morison provides us with a bit of fiction: "Coming to Boston with his father when over twenty years old, he entered Harvard College . . ." (p. 236). Taylor's father, of course, did not accompany the poet to New England. Taylor does not mention his father in the diary of the voyage.

[14]"The Marrow of Puritan Divinity," *Publications of the Colonial Society of Massachusetts*, XXXII (1938), 247-300.

[15]"Jonathan Edwards," *Literary History of the United States*, eds. Robert E. Spiller, et al. (New York, 1948), I, 74-75.

[16]"Writers of New England," *ibid.*, I, 66.

[17]*Literature and Theology in Colonial New England* (Cambridge, Mass., 1949), pp. 168-169.

[18]"Theology and Imagery in Taylor's Poetry," *NEQ*, XXVI (1953), 518-530.

[19]"Edward Taylor: A Revaluation," *NEQ*, XXI (1948), 518-530.

[20](Cambridge, Mass., 1953), p. 155.

[21]*The American Puritans* (New York, 1956), p. 302. On this same page Miller makes a number of mistakes concerning Taylor. He says that Taylor had seven children by his first wife; that Ezra Stiles deposited the manuscript of Taylor's poems unopened in the Yale Library; and that Taylor in his opposition to Stoddardeanism "appears to have confined his opposition to communings with himself." As a matter of fact, Taylor had eight children by his first wife; Ezra Stiles certainly opened the manuscript of Taylor's poems, for his signature is on an inside page; Ezra Stiles did not deposit the manuscript in the Yale Library—it was presented to Yale by Henry W. Taylor in 1883 many years after Stiles's death. Taylor did not keep his anti-Stoddardeanism to himself—he wrote a bitter letter to Stoddard on the subject. The letter is in Taylor's Commonplace Book now in the possession of the Massachusetts Historical Society.

[22]Johnson, *Poetical Works of Edward Taylor*, p. 182.

[23]*Ibid.*, p. 184.

[24]"Edward Taylor and the Cambridge Platonists," *AL*, XXVI (1954), 13.

DARWIN SHRELL

[1]*The Quest for Nationality: An American Literary Campaign* (Syracuse, 1957). In addition to this thorough and informative book, I am indebted to Harry Hayden Clark, "Literary Criticism in the *North American Review*," 1815-1835," *Wisconsin Academy of Sciences, Arts, and Letters*, XXXII (1940), 299-350; and Robert E. Streeter, "Association Psychology and Literary Nationalism in the *North American Review*," *AL*, XVII (November, 1945), 243-254.

[2]"Literary Delinquency in America," II (November, 1815), 35. Subsequent references in the *Review* will include only volume, issue, and page numbers.

[3]For a fuller discussion of the ideas in the romantic movement, see Arthur

O. Lovejoy, "On the Discrimination of Romanticisms," *Essays in the History of Ideas* (Baltimore, 1948), pp. 228-253.

[4]William H. Prescott, "English Literature of the Nineteenth Century," XXXV (July, 1832), 172; Oliver W. B. Peabody, "Sir Walter Scott," XXXIV (April, 1833), 289-315.

[5]Prescott, "English Literature of the Nineteenth Century," XXXV (1832), pp. 175-179.

[6]By 1850 the following reviewers had discussed Cooper in the *North American Review*: Lewis Cass, William H. Prescott, Francis Bowen, William H. Gardiner, Alexander S. Mackenzie, William Phillips, Grenville Mellen, and Oliver W. B. Peabody. Of these, William H. Gardiner was most completely in sympathy with Cooper's romanticisms, and Oliver W. B. Peabody was most strongly opposed.

[7]Streeter, "Association Psychology and Literary Nationalism . . .," pp. 243-254.

[8]*Ibid.*, p. 244.

[9]"Redwood, a Tale," XX (April, 1825), 271-272.

[10]"American Language and Literature," I, 313.

[11]"The Sylphs of the Seasons, with Other Poems," V (September, 1817), 365-389.

[12]Clark, "Literary Criticism in the *North American Review* . . .," pp. 299-350.

OTIS B. WHEELER

[1]T. L. Masson, "Emerson the Radical," *Bookman*, LVII (1923), 401-403; B. Hall, "Emerson the Anarchist," *Arena*, XXXVII (1907), 400-404; G. Shaw, "Emerson the Nihilist," *International Journal of Ethics*, XXV (1914), 68-86; E. C. Lindeman, "Emerson: Radical Democrat," *Common Ground*, II (1942), 3-6; John Dewey, "The Philosopher of Democracy," *International Journal of Ethics*, XIII (1903), 405-413.

[2]A. I. Ladu, "Emerson: Whig or Democrat?" *NEQ*, XIII (1940), 419-441.

[3]A. C. Kern, "Emerson and Economics," *NEQ*, XIII (1940), 678-696.

[4]Edward Waldo Emerson (ed.), *The Complete Works of Ralph Waldo Emerson* (Boston, 1903-1904), III, 209.

[5]*Ibid.*, II, 110.

[6]*Ibid.*, III, 209-210.

[7]Edward Waldo Emerson and Waldo Emerson Forbes (eds.), *The Journals of Ralph Waldo Emerson* (Boston, 1909-1914), VIII, 265.

[8]*Ibid.*, X, 228.

[9]Emerson (ed.), *Complete Works*, XI, 301.

[10]Emerson and Forbes (eds.), *Journals*, IX, 122.

[11]Emerson (ed.), *Complete Works*, III, 209-210.

[12]Quoted by Ralph L. Rusk, *The Life of Ralph Waldo Emerson* (New York, 1949), p. 368.

[13]Emerson and Forbes (eds.), *Journals*, VIII, 236.

[14]*Ibid.*, II, 141-142, 205.

[15]*Ibid.*, I, 311-312.

[16]*Ibid.*, IV, 85.

[17]*Ibid.*, V, 276.

[18]Emerson (ed.), *Complete Works*, II, 56.

[19]Emerson and Forbes (eds.), *Journals*, VII, 223.

[20]Emerson (ed.), *Complete Works*, IV, 246.

[21]Emerson and Forbes (eds.), *Journals*, VIII, 216.

[22]Emerson (ed.), *Complete Works*, VII, 13.

[23]Emerson and Forbes (eds.), *Journals*, IV, 410. The *Globe*, under the editorship of Francis Blair, was at this time the official organ of the Van Buren administration.

[24]Emerson (ed.), *Complete Works*, V. 304.

[25]Emerson and Forbes (eds.), *Journals*, II, 243.

[26]*Ibid.*, VII, 66.

[27]Rusk, *The Life of Ralph Waldo Emerson*, p. 289.

[28]Emerson (ed.), *Complete Works*, VI, 63-64.

[29]*Ibid.*, XI, 521.

[30]Emerson and Forbes (eds.), *Journals*, V, 423.

[31]*Ibid.*, II, 407-408.

[32]*Ibid.*, V, 76.

[33]*Ibid.*, IX, 335.

[34]*Ibid.*, VI, 446.

[35]*Ibid.*, VIII, 216.

[36]Emerson (ed.), *Complete Works*, IX, 223.

[37]*Ibid.*, pp. 398-399.

[38]Emerson and Forbes (eds.), *Journals*, VIII, 229.

[39]Quoted by Arthur M. Schlesinger, Jr., *The Age of Jackson* (Boston, 1946), pp. 295-296

LEWIS P. SIMPSON

[1]The history of the portraits and daguerreotypes of Poe is, like almost everything connected with his biography, complicated and uncertain. See Amanda Allan Poe, "Portraits and Daguerreotypes of Edgar Allan Poe," in *Facts About Poe* (Charlottesville, 1926), pp. 35-38. I am referring to the representation of Poe reproduced in Hervey Allen, *Israfel: the Life and Times of Edgar Allan Poe*, one volume edition (New York, 1934), p. 560.

[2]See the New York *Herald Tribune Book Review*, January 31, 1954, p. 1, for a reproduction of an engraving by A. H. Ritchie after the painting by Thomas Hicks.

[3]Hawthorne is depicted in the same pose, but I do not wish to become involved with Hawthorne's case in this discussion.

[4]This brief summary of the symbolic significance of the idea of the "Republic of Letters" is based on a study I have in progress. Although it does

not deal specifically with the concept of the Republic of Letters, I should like to call attention to one essay to which I am particularly indebted: William Phillips, "The Intellectuals' Tradition," *PR*, VIII (1941), 481-490.

[5]Louis Moland (ed.), *Oeuvres Complètes* (Paris, 1877-1885), XIV, 563-564.

[6]Peter Cunningham (ed.). *Works of Oliver Goldsmith* (London, 1854), II, 146.

[7]Cf. Lionel Trilling's comment on Baudelaire in "The Function of the Little Magazine," *The Liberal Imagination* (New York, 1954), p. 100.

[8]"Thoreau," *The Shock of Recognition*, ed. Edmund Wilson (New York, 1943), p. 236.

[9]*The Raven and the Whale: the War of Words and Wits in the Era of Poe and Melville* (New York, 1956), p. 7.

[10]Poe to Cooke, September 21, 1839, *The Letters of Edgar Allan Poe*, ed. John Ward Ostrom (Cambridge, Mass., 1948), II, 330. Hereinafter referred to as *Letters of Poe*.

[11]The entire "Prospectus" is reprinted in Arthur Hobson Quinn, *Edgar Allan Poe: a Critical Biography* (New York, 1941), pp. 306-308. It originally appeared in the Philadelphia *Saturday Courier*, X (June 13, 1840), 2.

[12]"Poe," *Shock of Recognition*, ed. Wilson, p. 7.

[13]"Our Cousin, Mr. Poe," *The Man of Letters in the Modern World* (New York, 1955), p. 140.

[14]Poe to Irving, June 21, 1841, *Letters of Poe*, I, 162.

[15]*Complete Works of Edgar Allan Poe*, James A. Harrison (ed.), (New York, 1902), XVI, 82.

[16]Poe to Snodgrass, April 1, 1841, *Letters of Poe*, I, 157.

[17]Quinn, *Poe*, p. 376. The "Prospectus" appeared originally in the Philadelphia *Saturday Museum*, March 4, 1843, p. 3.

[18]Poe, however, did not abandon the idea of "literature proper." The title page he designed for the *Stylus* describes it as a "Monthly Journal of Literature Proper, the Fine Arts, and the Drama." The title page is reproduced in Allen, *Israfel*, p. 589.

[19]Poe to Lowell, June 20, 1843, *Letters of Poe*, I, 234.

[20]*Id.* to *id.*, October 28, 1844, *Letters of Poe*, I, 266.

[21]*Id.* to Sarah J. Hale, January 16, 1846, *Letters of Poe*, II, 312.

[22]*Id.* to Patterson, April 30 (?), 1849, *Letters of Poe*, II, 443.

[23]*Id.* to *id.*, August 7, 1849, *Letters of Poe*, II, 457. See p. 458 for a note on Patterson's reply.

[24]*Id.* to Eveleth, June 26, 1849, *Letters of Poe*, II, 449-450.

[25]Cf. a comment on Poe and the New Criticism in Henry Nash Smith, "Can American Studies Develop a Method?" *AQ*, IX (1957), 203. Of course most of the New Critics have refused to recognize their descent from Poe, or at least to honor it. For a clear recognition of it, see George Snell, "First of the New Critics," *QR*, II (1946), 333-340.

NICHOLAS CANADAY, JR.

[1]See, e.g., Rosalie Feltenstein, "Melville's 'Benito Cereno,'" *AL*, XIX (1947), 245-255; Richard H. Fogle, "The Monk and the Bachelor: Melville's 'Benito Cereno,'" *TSE*, III (1952), 155-178; Joseph Schiffman, "Critical Problems in Melville's 'Benito Cereno,'" *MLQ*, XI (1950), 317-324; Stanley T. Williams, "Follow Your Leader: Melville's 'Benito Cereno,'" *VQR*, XXIII (1947), 65-76.

[2]The theme of authority as the organizing principle of Melville's fiction is the subect of Nicholas Canaday, Jr., "Melville and Authority: A Study of Thematic Unity" (Unpublished dissertation, University of Florida, 1957). Four major aspects of authority—the coercing power exercised by the ship captain, the state, society, and God—comprise a structural framework that affords a new approach to Melville's art and thought.

[3]Although Melville was concerned with rebellion against a ship captain's authority in each of his novels dealing with the sea, this is his only tale in which a mutiny is consummated. *Billy Budd*, which takes place in the year of the "Great Mutiny" (1797) in the British navy, derives much of its significance from the unrest of the fleet personnel in that year, but the Handsome Sailor is tried for murder in the course of a "mutinous act."

[4]Herman Melville, *Piazza Tales* (London, 1922), p. 70. Referenes throughout are to this edition and will subsequently appear in parentheses in the text.

[5]Melville's most authoritative sea captains are physically vigorous: Claret (*White Jacket*), Riga (*Redburn*), and Vere (*Billy Budd*). Even Captain Ahab, despite his scarred body, demonstrates a physical presence equal to that of any man aboard his ship. By contrast, the weak and vacillating Captain Guy (*Omoo*) is referred to by his sailors as "Paper Jack" because of his frail constitution.

[6]This principle of command is exaggerated to the point of caricature in *White Jacket* when the "high and mighty" commodore is portrayed in his magnificent aloofness. Captains Claret, Riga, and Vere meticulously avoid familiarity even with their subordinate officers, and Captain Ahab, by isolating himself in his cabin and refusing even the briefest human contacts, is nicknamed the "old Mogul" by his crew. Melville's narrator in *White Jacket* points out that the "mightiest potentates keep the most behind the veil."

[7]It is this trait of ingenuousness that is usually cited as the reason for Delano's mistaken appraisal of the situation aboard the Spanish vessel. It is pointed out, for example, that Delano "lacks the sense of evil" (Fogle, "The Monk and the Bachelor . . .," p. 159). A more serious charge is that "Captain Delano is moral simplicity in the form that borders upon weak-wittedness"; see Newton Arvin, *Herman Melville* (New York, 1950), p. 240. The present interpretation sees Delano's undistrustful nature as reinforcing his concept of a ship captain's absolute and unassailable authority.

[8]A critic who sees this tale as Melville's indictment of slavery observes that

Delano's mistake arises because he "suffers a mental block in looking at Negroes" and "cannot conceive of them as fully rounded people," but believes them to be "quite happy as slaves and servants" (Schiffman, "Critical Problems . . .," p. 322) . Such a judgment is too severe. Captain Delano's mental block is that he cannot conceive of any power aboard a ship outside of the captain's authority.

⁹The present interpretation seeks to refute the charge that the concluding legal document is either a "serious technical fault" or indicates that the manuscript was sold in incomplete form. See Geoffrey Stone, *Melville* (New York, 1944), p. 220; Leon Howard, *Herman Melville* (Berkeley, 1951) , p. 222.

¹⁰The empty scabbard has been cited as pointing to the "disintegration of Spanish grandeur of the past" (Williams, "Follow Your Leader . . .," p. 70) . Similarly, order has been recognized as an important theme, but the "order of Spain, an hierarchical system in which Church and State are one" (Fogle, "The Monk and the Bachelor . . .," p. 164) . The swordless scabbard has more immediate significance as a symbol of powerless authority, but the authority of the ship captain is, of course, a specific aspect of a larger concept of order.

HARRY OSTER

¹Stith Thompson, *The Folktale* (New York, 1946) , pp. 8-9.

²Cotton Mather, *Magnalia Christi Americana,* ed. Thomas Robbins (Hartford, 1853) , II, 620-623.

³John Greenleaf Whittier, *The Works of John Greenleaf Whittier* (Boston, 1892) , I, 270. Hereinafter cited as *Works*.

⁴Stith Thompson, *Motif-Index of Folk Literature* (Bloomington, 1955).

⁵For an early treatment by Whittier of this same supernatural subject, see "The Spectre Warriors," *The Legends of New England* (Hartford, 1831) , p. 76.

⁶*Ibid.,* p. 86.

⁷Mather, *Magnalia,* ed. Robbins, I, 84.

⁸*Essex Gazette,* May 1, 1830, p. 2.

⁹Joseph Dow, *History of Hampton* (Salem, 1893) , I, 80.

¹⁰*Works,* IV, 235.

¹¹*Ibid.,* p. 239.

¹²Dow, *History of Hampton,* I, 55.

¹³*Works,* IV, 258-259.

¹⁴*Ibid.,* I, 360.

¹⁵*Ibid.,* p. 367.

¹⁶For additional writing by Whittier on the subject of witches, see "The Weird Gathering," *Legends of New England,* p. 15; "Mabel Martin," *Works,* I, 195; and "The Haunted House," *Legends of New England,* p. 56.

¹⁷*Works,* I, 75.

¹⁸Samuel Adams Drake, *A Book of New England Legends* (Boston, 1910) , pp. 391-392.

[19]*Works*, I, 76.

[20]Kenneth Scott, "The Source of Whittier's *The Dead Ship of Harpswell*," *American Neptune*, VI (1946), 224.

[21]*Ibid.*, p. 225.

[22]Charles M. Skinner, *Myths and Legends of Our Land* (Philadelphia, 1896), p. 180.

[23]*Works*, IV, 272-273.

[24]Quoted by Jules Zanger, "A Note on Skipper Ireson's Ride," *NEQ*, XXIX (1956), 238.

[25]Quoted by E. E. Ericson, "John Hort and Skipper Ireson," *NEQ*, X (1937), 531-532.

[26]B. A. Botkin, *A Treasury of New England Folklore* (New York, 1947), p. 524.

[27]Samuel Roads, Jr., *The History and Traditions of Marblehead* (Marblehead, 1880), pp. 292-295.

[28]*Works*, I, 174-175.

[29]*Ibid.*, p. 178.

[30]Quoted by B. A. Botkin, *A Treasury of Southern Folklore* (New York, 1949), p. 235.

[31]*Ibid.*, p. 235.

[32]*Ibid.*, p. 236.

[33]Samuel T. Pickard, *Life and Letters of John Greenleaf Whittier* (Boston, 1894), I, 454-456.

[34]*Ibid.*, p. 457.

[35]*Ibid.*, p. 459.

[36]*Ibid.*, p. 458.

JOHN ROLAND DOVE

[1]Rebecca West, *Henry James* (London, 1916), pp. 69-70; Oscar Cargill, "*The Portrait of a Lady*: A Critical Reappraisal," *MFS*, III (1957), 29; Quentin Anderson, *The American Henry James* (New Burnswick, N. J., 1957), p. 197.

[2]All references in parentheses in the text are to The Modern Library Edition (New York, 1951).

[3]See also F. O. Matthiessen, *Henry James: The Major Phase* (Oxford, 1944), pp. 179-180; F. W. Dupee, *Henry James* (New York, 1951), p. 125.

[4]For an excellent summary of various conjectures, see Cargill, "*The Portrait of a Lady* . . .," pp. 24-26.

THOMAS C. RUMBLE

[1]Grover Smith, Jr., *T. S. Eliot's Poetry and Plays: A Study in Sources and Meaning* (Chicago, 1956), p. 18. Professor Smith's book appeared after the present paper was written for presentation at the 1956 meeting of the South-Central Modern Language Association, but I am pleased to note that there are several points concerning the "Prufrock" poem upon which, entirely for-

tuitously, we have reached quite similar conclusions. Smith views the structure of the poem, for example, much as I do when he comments that it contains "traces of a medieval débat, as in 'The Body and the Soul' " (p. 16) .

² (New York, 1920) .

³ *The Quest of the Holy Grail* (London, 1913) , p. 28.

⁴ The only edition of *Diu Crône*, ed. G. H. F. Scholl (Stuttgart, 1852), is long out of print. Jessie Weston gives a translation of the Grail episode of this romance in *Sir Gawain at the Grail Castle*, No. VI of the series, *Arthurian Romances Unrepresented in Malory's Morte d'Arthur* (London, 1902) , pp. 33-46.

⁵ *The Waste Land*, 11. 187-190. Eliot's poetry is quoted from *Collected Poems, 1909-1935* (New York, 1936) .

⁶ William Frost (ed.) , *Modern Poetry* (New York, 1950) , p. 111, note to 1. 14.

⁷ The suggestion here of a potential fertility which lapses finally into fruitlessness parallels perfectly the steady pattern of Prufrock's psychological advance and withdrawal throughout the poem.

⁸ The resignation implicit in Prufrock's reluctance to "disturb" this universe of his, in which "the afternoon, the evening, sleeps so peacefully" (1. 75) , is echoed later in the opening lines of *The Waste Land*:

April is the cruelest month, breeding
Lilacs out of the dead land, mixing
Memory and desire, stirring
Dull roots with spring rain.

These lines, of course, are meant to stand in ironic contrast to the typical medieval poet's introductory convention of welcoming spring and the rebirth of all things, both natural and spiritual. The opening lines of the Prologue to *The Canterbury Tales* furnish the best-known example.

⁹ 11. 17-22. The imagery here is considerably more complex than I have implied. It involves not only the actual scene of Prufrock in a tearoom and the ironically corresponding figure of the questing Grail knight in the chamber of the Fisher King, but suggests as well a church scene in which congregational questions are "dropped upon a plate" that is passed for this specific purpose and in which "the taking of a toast and tea" represents some final affirmation of one's communion with God. It is the reluctance of Eliot's world to drop its questions, to reach some kind of affirmation, which Eliot seems to see, both here and in *The Waste Land*, as the greatest contributing factor to the spiritual sterility of his age.

¹⁰ 11. 73-74. There is something more here, too, than just Prufrock's despairing acknowledgment of defeat. Eliot implies, I think, that there is, after all, some modicum of good in Prufrock's introspective experience. George Williamson in *A Reader's Guide to T. S. Eliot* (New York, 1955) , p. 127, comments that in *The Waste Land* "the Fisher King is differentiated from the Phoenician Sailor by his awareness of the *means* of transcendence (of this

physical world) ." There is also something of this in Prufrock's despair: the body and soul of Prufrock's double self become throughout the poem progressively differentiated by some basic awareness on his part of at least "the *means* of transcendence," however unable he is, finally, to act in terms of that awareness.

[11]See the Welsh story, "Peredur the Son of Evrawc," *The Mabinogion*, tr. Lady Charlotte Guest (London, 1906), pp. 176-219.

[12]*Hamlet*, III:i, 76-82.

[13]XXVII, 61-66. The translation is mine.

[14]*Hamlet*, III:i, 85-88.

[15]11. 129-131. Compare this ending to the ending of Gawain's guest in Gautier's continuation of Chrétien de Troyes' *Perceval*, in Weston tr., *Sir Gawain at the Grail Castle*, pp. 3-30. In Gautier's version Gawain is partially successful in his quest: he asks the Grail King about the bleeding lance and about the Sword of the Dolorous Stroke, thus partially restoring fertility to the waste kingdom; but before asking the final, crucial question concerning the Grail service, he falls asleep. While he sleeps he is transported in a cart from this Grail chamber in the sea to the shore nearby; and he is awakened in the morning by the "human voices" of a blighted people, who both bless and curse him—the one for his partial success, the other for his failure to succeed completely.

BERNARD BENSTOCK

[1]All parenthetical numbers in the text are page references to Cummings, *Poems (1923-1954)* (New York, 1954), containing all ten volumes of poetry.

JAMES L. ROBERTS

[1]In addition to *Light in August* (1932), he had also published such outstanding novels as *Sartoris* (1929), *The Sound and the Fury* (1929), *As I Lay Dying* (1930), *Sanctuary* (1931), and the short stories collected in the volume *These Thirteen* (1931), which contain such stories as "A Rose for Emily," "Dry September," "That Evening Sun," "Red Leaves," and "A Justice."

[2]Some of these themes have been developed by critics, especially man's isolation in the modern world by Irwin Howe; *William Faulkner: A Critical Study* (New York, 1951), pp. 148-151; man's responsibility to the community by Cleanth Brooks, "Notes on Faulkner's *Light in August*," *Harvard Advocate*, CXXXV (1951), 10-11, 27; the sacrifice of Christ by C. Hugh Holman, "The Unity of Faulkner's *Light in August*," *PMLA*, LXXXIII (1958), 155-166; and man's inhumanity to man by Phyllis Hirshleifer, "As Whirlwinds in the South: An Analysis of *Light in August*," *Per, II* (1949), 225-238.

[3]Richard Chase in his essay "The Stone and Crucifixion: Faulkner's *Light in August*," *William Faulkner: Two Decades of Criticism*, ed. Frederick J. Hoffman and Olga W. Vickery (East Lansing, Mich., 1951), pp. 205-217, maintains that the "curve image stands for holistic consciousness, a contain-

ing culture and tradition, the cyclical life and death of all the creatures of earth." He does not, however, see this same image as being applicable to the affirmation of the other characters in the novel, but rather, the cause of their defeat.

⁴All quotations are from the Modern Library Edition of *Light in August* (New York, 1950). All parenthetical numbers in the text are page references to this work.

⁵To Joe, urns were symbolic of disorder (p. 165) and he destroyed all the urns which contained liquor before murdering Joanna Burden (p. 98).

⁶"The Stone and Crucifixion . . .," *Two Decades of Criticism*, eds. Hoffman and Vickery, pp. 206-207.

⁷"As Whirlwinds in the South . . .," pp. 225-238.

⁸"Notes on Faulkner's *Light in August*," pp. 10-11, 27.

⁹*Ibid.*, p. 11.

¹⁰"As Whirlwinds in the South . . .," p. 230.

¹¹There may be one exception. When Percy Grimm kills Joe Christmas, the other members of the posse, who were coerced into following Grimm, become nauseated at Grimm's atrocity.

¹²Until the final pages of the novel, Hightower can never bring into a complete unity the two divergent accounts of his grandfather's death. He delights in the account of his grandfather being shot from a horse while brandishing his sword during Van Dorn's cavalry raid, and also in the more realistic account of his grandfather being killed by a shotgun while stealing chickens. The last account, given by Cindy, the Negro slave, finally succeeds in becoming the realistic view as Hightower attains a more rational grasp of life.

¹³Many of Hightower's characteristics may be viewed in Faulkner's earlier characterizations, especially in Horace Benbow in *Sanctuary* and Jason Compson III in *The Sound and the Fury*. Hightower's ineffectual attempts to save Joe Christmas may be aptly compared to Horace's equally ineffectual efforts to save Goodwin. His tendency to isolate himself and detach himself from the outer world may be noted in Jason Compson III.

¹⁴"Thematic Design in *Light in August*," *SAQ*, LIII (1954), 544.

¹⁵This statement about the mixed blood of Sam Fathers in "The Old People," *Go Down, Moses* (1955), p. 168, is equally applicable to Joe Christmas.

¹⁶There is also the implication of a more religious interpretation that if Christmas has no Negro blood, then he can no longer be a part of God's chosen people. "The curse of the black race is God's curse. But the curse of the White race is the black man who will be forever God's chosen own because he once cursed him."

¹⁷The Christian myth in this passage with the baptismal ritual, the struggle comparable to Christ's struggle before the crucifixion, the night in the barn (or manger) is not used necessarily to suggest that Christmas is the Christ figure, but rather to deepen Christmas' internal struggle by suggesting as an

analogy the depth of Christ's struggle before His crucifixion, thus intensifying Christmas' struggle.

[18]Holman, "The Unity of . . . *Light in August*," p. 157, views this episode as "the day of the Holy Week on which Christ cleansed the temple."

[19]Old Doc Hines' desire for his grandson's death can be taken on one level as the desire of a typical fanatic for white supremacy. His wildness is a result of his smallness; "and he had to fight because he is littler than most men . . . that was his vanity and his pride." But his fanaticism becomes significant when applied to his own grandson, because this emphasizes Christmas' isolation from society; he can never be accepted when his own grandfather rejects him. And again, on a religious level, Hines could possibly be viewed as the Godhead, and then his rejection of Christmas makes man the complete victim of hostile forces. This analogy would then intensify Christmas' conflict, and his struggle becomes the struggle of all mankind against the hostile forces of the universe.

[20]The destruction of the black and the survival of the white is interestingly pointed by the fact that Hightower delivers only two children, a black one who dies and the white one of Lena who survives.

[21]Introduction, *The Portable Faulkner*, ed. Malcolm Cowley (New York, 1946), p. 18; and Howe, *William Faulkner*, pp. 149, 153.

[22]This is basically the same theme that Faulkner uses in *A Fable*; i.e., if Christ were to return to the world today, he would have to be crucified again.

[23]For some of the various Christian symbols, see Beckman W. Cottrell, "Christian Symbol in 'Light in August,'" *MFS*, II (1956-57), 207-213. Mr. Cottrell imposes a Christian allegory upon the novel, using Joanna Burden (initials J. B.) as John the Baptist because she was beheaded, Byron as Joseph because of his "ever-present mule," and other parallels. For other Christian symbols, see Holman, "The Unity of . . . *Light in August*," pp. 155-156.

HORACE TAYLOR

[1]The history of critical work on *The Heart Is a Lonely Hunter* is curious. The work received five highly favorable reviews at its publication: New York *Herald Tribune Books*, June 23, 1940, p. 11; *NYTBR*, June 16, 1940, p. 6; New York *World Telegram*, July 1, 1940, p. 12; *NY*, XVI (July 8, 1940), pp. 77-8; *Saturday Review of Literature*, XXII (July 1, 1940), p. 6. Since that time the book has only rarely been dealt with. The following seem to be the principal studies: Anon., "Human Isolation," *TLS*, No. 2685, July 17, 1953, p. 460; Frédéric I. Carpenter, "The Adolescent in American Fiction," *EJ*, XLVI (1957), pp. 313-319; Frank Durham, "God and No God in *The Heart Is a Lonely Hunter*," *SAQ*, LVI (1957), pp. 494-499.

[2]Though the setting of *The Heart Is a Lonely Hunter* is highly generalized with few local details that seem to tie it to any particular place, the author probably based it on Columbus, Georgia. Some of the the local details such

as the New York Café appear to be taken from the town. But a more import-- tant reason for believing that the town of *The Heart Is a Lonely Hunter*, for all its generalized quality, is based on Columbus is the fact that Carson Mc- Cullers was born there, has lived much of her life there, and is still consid- ered a local celebrity.

Contributors

BENSTOCK, BERNARD, b. New York, New York, 1930; A. B., Brooklyn College, 1950; A. M., Columbia University, 1954; Ph. D., Florida State University, 1957; Assistant, Florida State University, 1955-1957; Instructor, Louisiana State University, 1957-; contributor to *The Explicator.*

CANADAY, NICHOLAS, Jr., b. New York, New York, 1928; A.B., Princeton University, 1950; University of London, 1949; M. A., University of Florida, 1955, Ph. D., 1957; Instructor, The Bolles School, 1952-54, Commandant of Cadets, 1952-54, Assistant Principal, 1953-54; Assistant, University of Florida, 1954-57; Instructor, Louisiana State University, 1957-59, Assistant Professor, 1959-.

DOVE, JOHN ROLAND, b. London, England, 1924; B. A. Oxford, 1949, M. A., 1955; Ph. D., University of Texas, 1956; Instructor in Western Civilization, Hobart College, 1949-51; Instructor, University of Texas, 1953-56; Instructor, Louisiana State University, 1956-58, Assistant Professor, 1958-; author of articles in University of Texas *Studies in English.*

OSTER, HARRY, b. Cambridge, Massachusetts, 1923; B. A., Harvard University, 1946; M. B. A., Columbia University, 1948; M. A. Cornell University, 1950, Ph. D., 1953; Fellow, Cornell University, 1950-53; Instructor, Louisiana State University, 1955-57, Assistant Professor, 1957-; Friends of Music Scholarship, Cornell University, 1952; Fellow, Ford Education Forum, 1956; three grants from Research Council of Louisiana State University; co-founder and first Secretary of Louisiana Folklore Society; papers read for Folklore Institute of Indiana University, Ohio Folklore Society, American Folklore Society, Louisiana Folklore Society, and South-Central Modern Language Association; lecture-concerts dealing with folk music and the songs of Robert Burns given at various colleges and on radio and television; author of articles in *New York Folklore Quarterly, Louisiana Folklore Miscellany, Notre Damean,* and *McNeese Review;* 13 albums of folk music published by Louisiana Folklore Society, Folkways, Lyricon, and Folk-Lyric Recording Co.

ROBERTS, JAMES L., b. Webb, Mississippi, 1929; B. S., Memphis State University, 1950; M. A., University of Mississippi, 1954; Ph. D., University of

Iowa, 1957; Assistant, University of Iowa, 1954-57; Instructor, Louisiana State University, 1957-58; Instructor, University of Colorado, 1958-; contributor to *Abstracts of English Studies*.

RUMBLE, THOMAS C., b. Deckerville, Michigan, 1919; B. A. Tulane University, 1949, M. A., 1951, Ph. D., 1955; Assistant, Tulane University, 1949-51; Instructor, University of Mississippi, 1951-53; Instructor, Tulane Unversity, 1953-55; Instructor, Louisiana State University, 1955-57, Assistant Professor, 1957-59; Assistant Professor, Wayne State University, 1959-, Carnegie Fellowship, 1955; grant, Research Council of Louisiana State University, 1957; President, Philological Club of Louisiana State University, 1957-58; Secretary, English Section I, South-Central Modern Language Association, 1959-60; author of articles in *Modern Language Notes*, *Modern Language Quarterly*, *Journal of English and Germanic Philology*, and *Comparative Literature*.

SHRELL, DARWIN, b. Oak Grove, Louisiana, 1917; B. A., Louisiana Polytechnic Institute, 1939; M. A., University of Texas, 1948, Ph. D., 1951; Instructor, University of Texas, 1950-52; Visiting Professor, North Alabama State College, summer 1951; Visiting Professor, Northern Michigan State College, 1952-53; Instructor, Louisiana State University, 1953-56, Assistant Professor, 1956-; Visiting Professor, Northern Michigan State College, summer 1957; Fellowship, University of Texas, 1948; President, Louisiana Folklore Society, 1957-58; Secretary, American Literature Section I, South-Central Modern Language Association, 1956-57, Chairman, 1957-58; Editor, *Louisiana Folklore Miscellany*, 1959.

SIMPSON, LEWIS, P., b. Jacksboro, Texas, 1916; B. A., University of Texas, 1938, M. A., 1939, Ph. D., 1948; Instructor, University of Texas, 1941-42, 1944-48; Assistant Professor, Louisiana State University, 1948-53, Associate Professor, 1953-; Fellowship, University of Texas, 1939-40, Advanced Fellowship, 1946; two grants from Research Council of Louisiana State University; Guggenheim Fellow, 1954-55; Chairman, American Literature Section I, South-Central Modern Language Association, 1955-56; Secretary, General Topics, South-Central Modern Language Association, 1955-56, Chairman, 1956-57; papers read for South-Central Modern Language Association, Philological Club of Louisiana State University, Louisiana College Conference, Modern Language Association, American Literature Club of Louisiana State University, Texas American Studies Association, English Department Lecture Series of Louisiana State University; author of reviews in *American Literature* and Baton Rouge *Morning Advocate*, and articles in *Library Chronicle of the University of Texas*, *New England Quarterly*, *Boston Public Library Quarterly*, and *Emerson Society Quarterly*.

STANFORD, DONALD E., b. Amherst, Massachusetts, 1913; A. B., Stanford University, 1933, Ph. D., 1953; M. A., Harvard University, 1934; Instructor, Colorado State College, 1935-37; Instructor, Dartmouth College, 1937-41;

Instructor, University of Nebraska, 1941-42; Instructor, U. S. Air Corps, 1942-45; Instructor, Brazilian Air Corps, 1945-48; Instructor, New Haven Junior College, 1948-49; Instructor, Louisiana State University, 1949-50, Assistant Professor, 1953-56, Associate Professor, 1956-; W. D. Briggs Scholarship, Stanford University, 1935, Royall Victor Scholarship, Guggenheim Fellow, 1959-60; author of poems in *Poetry, Hound and Horn, The Magazine, Harvard Advocate, New Republic, Commonweal, Talisman,* and several anthologies; articles and reviews in Baton Rouge *Morning Advocate, Southern Review, Kenyon Review, Poetry, American Literature, Twentieth Century Literature, Talisman, Yale Library Gazette, New York History.* Author of *New England Earth,* 1941; *The Traveler,* 1955.

TAYLOR, HORACE P., Jr., b. Jacksonville, Florida, 1927; B. A., Stetson University, 1952, M. A. 1955; Assistant, Stetson University, 1952-53; Assistant, Louisiana State University, 1955-58, Instructor, 1958-59; Instructor, McNeese State College, 1959-60.

WHEELER, OTIS, b. Mansfield, Arkansas, 1921; B. A., University of Oklahoma, 1942; M. A., University of Texas, 1947; Ph. D., University of Minnesota, 1951; Tutor, University of Texas, 1946-47; Assistant, University of Minnesota, 1948-50; Instructor, Louisiana State University, 1952-54, Assistant Professor, 1954-; author of articles in *American Literature* and *Nineteenth Century Fiction.*